WOMEN IN A
GOLDEN STATE

Published by Gunpowder Press
Edited by David Starkey and Chryss Yost
PO Box 60035
Santa Barbara, CA 93160-0035

Cover: Mary Heebner, www.maryheebner.com, *I've heard the mermaids sing*, Handmade paper collage 2022

ISBN-13: 978-1-957062-23-5

Library of Congress Control Number: 2025905541

www.gunpowderpress.com

Gunpowder Press is part of Gunpowder Poetry, a 501(c)(3) nonprofit literary organization.

WOMEN IN A GOLDEN STATE

CALIFORNIA POETS AT 60 AND BEYOND

EDITED BY

DIANA RAAB & CHRYSS YOST

GUNPOWDER PRESS • SANTA BARBARA
2025

Women in a Golden State emerged during a dinnertime brainstorming session between the two of us. Diana had recently celebrated her 70th birthday and was reflecting on her first college paper, "Aging Gracefully." Chryss, a lifelong California getting close to 60, was well past identifying as one of the Beach Boys' "California Girls." We were both feeling anxious and eager to find a new project. Maybe a collection of poems?

California's namesake, the warrior queen Calafia, emerged from a poem over five hundred years ago. A Castillian poet imagined Califia as a fierce leader, leading an army of women in a legendary kingdom. Our State's literary queens include Joan Didion and Octavia Butler, one born in Sacramento, one born in Pasadena. Many of the writers in this collection were born elsewhere, bringing outside influences with them to add to the ongoing mixtape of California literary culture. In the 1960s and -70s, television offered up *Gidget* or *The Brady Bunch* or *Charlie's Angels*. But then what? Where did California girls go next?

This emerged as our focus: the mythology and reality of being a woman of a certain age, especially in youth-obsessed California. This anthology invites readers to reconsider aging not as an end, but as an ongoing journey—one filled with beauty, strength, and boundless possibilities. Through a diverse array of voices and experiences, *Women in a Golden State* highlights the rich and varied lives and perspectives of older women, proving that age is no barrier to achievement, creativity, or relevance.

When we put out the call for submissions, we received poems and micro-essays from hundreds of poets and writers across California. The influences in this collection come from Hollywood and Haight-Ashbury, they stretch into the Mojave and the Sierras, and across Humboldt's forests to the Salton Sea.

The year 2025 marks the 175th anniversary of California's statehood, so we decided to choose 175 contributors. We wanted to capture a wide range of voices, not necessarily the most published or highly lauded. We limited our selections to one piece per writer and selected writing which felt to us to capture a certain truth. Our selections include Poets Laureate side-by-side with writers who are just discovering their literary voices. California serves as a fitting backdrop for this anthology—a state known for its diversity, reinvention, and creativity. Just as the landscape ranges from rugged coastlines to serene deserts, so do these poems transverse the emotional terrain of aging women.

Women in a Golden State is a poetic celebration of resilience, wisdom, and transformation, a platform for women in California over the age of 60 to share their unique life perspectives. This anthology gathers a vibrant collection of emerging and well-published voices reflecting on the passage of time, the beauty of lived experiences, those "Eureka!" moments, and the challenges and triumphs that come with age. Diana's poem "Create a Revolution" captures this spirit:

Create a Revolution

Incite change,
look for a patch
of difficulty amongst glistening clouds,
hunt for an need unmet,
or a journey you want to take.

Stretch your arms to the sky's glow,
find peace within yourself
tap into the closet never opened

and pull down old journals
written before wrinkled foreheads
and children expanding like
spiders crafting their webs.

Sink your teeth into good books,
write the author to share your bliss
for their warm words
which hold the oldest of bones

in your family all gone,
as you sit in your senior position
the same way you were once the youngest
and most boisterous of all.

Teach the world how life circles
and how change never really occurs
it just begs for a new sunlight.

Let yourself go
be the one who
they all talk about
when you are gone.

Our hope is that you enjoy this collection as much as we enjoyed putting it together. Thank you to our literary mothers who have inspired and guided us, as well as our mothers and grandmothers who raised us to love books. Thanks to David Starkey, the founding publisher of Gunpowder Press. We are grateful to live in a community of gifted writers, including many in these pages—their inspiration and encouragement is essential. We are both fortunate to have loving and patient partners who understand the creative process; Simon Raab and George Yatchisin, thank you.

CONTENTS

Farther Along

Farther along we'll know all about it
Yes, we'll understand it all by and by

When I visit my family's cabin in the San Bernardino mountains, I hike down the Santa Ana river, along the scoured and ragged shoreline emerging months after tropical storm Hilary, looking for old landmarks. Gone are the sandy banks, the oak shade spots with carpets of acorn. Where is the rock where I laid the sleeping baby down? The deep swimming hole where I swam with friends? The tree with the tire swing that someone, not me, mended yearly?

At its peak, the late summer storm widened the river to seven times its width. The raging water took down mature cedars, pines, and oaks, stripping them of branches and bark, leaving them tumbled and tangled in vast stacks. I won't live long enough to see trees return to the river's once heavily forested banks.

Some felled trees and boulders wear clothes and bedding, rocks wrapped with curtains, towels and rugs. The raging water took homes along with the trees. Sunk deep in the dirt and branches is the stuff that makes up lives: pillows, shoes, utensils, appliances, furniture. People say those who stayed behind took refuge in the trees that August night, watching their homes vanish. All but one survived. That missing woman, not much older than me, living alone in a mobile home, swept away, haunts me. She stayed, some say, because she had nowhere else to go or no way to get there. There's always a point, thinking of her, where she used to be, where she may be now, that keeps me from walking even farther.

That was last year. This year, a fire came and burned for almost a month. Some of the very trees that survived the flood, stand as ashy skeletons now. The river is edged with soot. No one has yet found her.

Warrior Spirit

I come from a line of women, strong
Enduring women, who
Swallowed befallen wrongs
Held tight the hammer
Cracked the cement wall that contained them

I come from a line of women, secrets
Built that wall
Broke their hearts
Let them grow cold,
Let them break ties with the past,
Hid them from fame
Beauty unrecognized
Dried, as thistles, sharp seeds
Hid warrior spirits

I come from a line of women warriors
Acknowledge the gift
Plant the seeds
Sing the stories
Reject silence for justice
Step forward breaking free

Time Stamp

Long overdue, a deep clean
of my Honda Accord yields
this relic from the ashtray:
a parking pass stamped 2.2.03,
11:58 am, Paseo Nuevo Mall.
Lunchtime, a rendezvous
confirmed by my datebook—
Pascucci's with my good
friend Margy. An Italian
chopped salad, a swing
by Macy's or Nordstrom
afterward—TGIF after
a long week of work,
at a time when I worked
hard and couldn't stop.
Later that year I'd be struck
by cancer, my reality
altered forever. This ticket
survived in secret, moved
with me to the Mojave,
surfaced at this late date—
a white flag of truce
from my former life,
ready for recycling.

Even the Land...

Sometimes, even the land forgets.
In fire change happens immediately, drastically:
bridges leveled, buildings gone,
trees twisted into charred black skeletons,
fading remains of memory.

Part of nature's cycle,
fire provides a brutal cleansing,
a path of destruction making way
for the creation of something new.

When I first learned of the blaze
I was traveling with my soon-to-be ex.
From our tiny loft we pondered
what would become of the hot spring
where we spent our first vacation
camped out in separate tents
two decades ago.

We returned as our relationship lay
In smoldering ruins,
hanging on to desperate memory,
as the Spring foretold us of
conflagrations to come.

If I could revisit the Spring as it was,
I'd rejoice in that romance,
stroll blissfully past the funky dormitories,
and meditation pavilion in my younger body
finally appreciating things so readily lost,
yet not noticed until no longer there.

In youth we presume structures will endure,
love will always be available
and that our lives are infinite.

But sometimes, even the land remembers
what the mind forgets;
that the body is fragile and time is a firestorm,
obliterating what we once assumed.
was ours forever.

Notes from an Outsider

Your claim to Laguna is justified. You live here. I don't. You pay taxes. You do community work and take care of your neighbors. You grocery shop here and drive your kids to the local school. You keep your bushes trimmed and keep your birdfeeders full. You have lived here for years. You grew up here. You may have inherited your sweet beach cottage or worked crazy hard to buy it.

I suspect you earned your status in this renowned artist community. Over the years, with hard work and discipline, you developed your craft. You exhibit in the local galleries. You swim in Laguna beaches. You know every hidden cove. You buy Girl Scout cookies. Your kids play in the playgrounds. You taught your teen to drive a stick on its hills. You exercise in its clubs and hike its wooded paths. Laguna is your home. Not mine.

But can you share it with me this afternoon? I wish I lived here. Who wouldn't want to just open a window for an ocean breeze on any day and gaze at the simmering blue sea? Who wouldn't want to take an after-work dip in the waves, without driving the God-awful 55 freeway for hours? If I had more time in my day or more space in my house, I'd bring out my oils from the garage and play around with them. Once, I was told I had potential in art. My kids would be lean and strong and maybe co-operative. If they lived here, I bet they would thrive. Neighbors would smile. It would be safe to have a lemonade stand.

Anyway.... I digress. If I could just cool off, have a beer, take a swim, play on the sand with my kids, I'd feel a lot better.

Never to Be Seen Again

Unable to live on earth, Mira ventured out alone in the sky
—Mirabai

I could die right here on this outcropping of land,
sitting cross-legged on a cliff above the estuary
of an earthquake fault; here on the edge of Little
Mesa overlooking the Pacific, Bolinas Bay, and its
convergence with the lagoon. No one need take
notice: distant surfers are busy with the waves;
people far below me on the sand play with their
dogs or walk, heads bowed, looking for rocks,
sea glass, or shells. The brilliant pink ice plant
flowers surrounding me are surprisingly soft,
they could decorate my funeral pyre—only I don't
want to go up in flames—just a miraculous
disappearing will do, like the mystic poet Mirabai
whose crumpled clothes they found on the ground
one morning in the Krishna temple after all-night
passionate prayers [her body never to be seen
again]. Yes, I could disappear right here, even
the vultures will forget their efficient circling
. . . just this view, and the welcoming sky will do
to guide me on my way, and maybe the old canoe
beached below might make an eulogistic crossing
of the channel I gaze upon leading to the sea
where sharks eye seals [those whiskered angels]
and the tide swoons ceaselessly to the moon.

As Long as She Likes

On the way to the cemetery, I slept.
Not in the limousine that carried my mother's coffin
but out cold in a van, the family all talking around me.
I was exhausted from her suffering, her pleas—
help me and *enough, enough*—
and trying to get the morphine to stay in the ditch of her gums.
How could I not have studied this in advance?
The way my mother learned to give shots in nursing school,
plunging the needle into an orange
then practicing on the other girls.
God only gives you strength for one day at a time.
How many times did I hear her say this?
Ask yourself, can I make this day?
And then she made her last day.
On the way back, the driver got lost. As we circled unfamiliar
fields and trees dizzy with blossoms, we began to imagine
we could buy some land.
Horses. A lake. Everything seemed possible.
And hilarious. We were a little hysterical,
driving into the luxury of the future.
I've never returned to my mother's grave.
But I see her every day. Here she is in short boots,
coming back from the beach with a jar of seawater.
Each morning she feeds me a spoonful. Minerals.
It's something she read in the *Pleasantville Press*.
Here she's wrapping pints and quarts in that same paper,
sliding them into brown bags.
She's counting out coins into the customer's hands,
careful to touch their palms.
And here in her bathrobe on a Saturday night. The store just closed.
She bites into a hoagie, steak and onions, sips a beer.
Tomorrow morning she can sleep late. There's a law
in New Jersey that liquor stores have to close on Sunday.
A blessed law that lets my mother sleep...
and then sit down with a cigarette and black coffee,
one strong leg crossed over the other.
She can sit there as long as she likes.

Sage

If I have you
In every room of this house
A place long benighted
Will I then be able to pass my hand
Over counterpane and countertop
Over Grandma's chair
This wall
This windowsill
Like Queen Christina
Lingering at every fresh memory made

Can I ignite you
Burn you as a tight bundle of green sage
Trail your cleansing volatile smoke
Slowly
Deliberately
A skein of dark silk
Transparent
Astringent
Chasing out what was
Opening to the scent of rain

Mountain Lion

for my Granddaughter

Your dad drove past her body three times on the freeway.
He finally stopped in the dark.
Headlights flashed past as he rolled the lion onto the silver tarp,
        hefted her into his car.

His call tore us from sleep.
We consented to the delivery.
In the cold night we viewed her body in the back seat—
paws the size of a child's fist, ear scarred from a fight, tail wider than a rope.

Awkward pallbearers, we carried her through the house at midnight
angled the heavy tarp down polished wooden stairs under sharp electric glare,
through the glass door's black reflection.

We laid her in moonlight on the porch.
Her fur was soft, brownish.
She was juvenile perhaps but 80 pounds at least.
Her stomach round and soft too – maybe newly pregnant.
Her neck was snapped, jaw broken, a hole torn deep in the flesh,
the wound a neat little vent, red and purple organs visible.

Alone he bore her to the frosted yard, to leave her body there till morning.

While after Christmas, your friends flew pink winged ponies,
shrieked on scooters, gamed on pixelated, beeping screens,
you studied the dead lion, touched her, talked quietly.
From the porch I watched you disappear into the forest.
You followed as he carried her and laid her in the hole he dug –
deeper than your knees, you said.
With your hands you helped spread the mud, redwood duff, fern fronds
so only you two knew where.

To the White Pine, Mono Lake

We met after a week's camping in Nevada, stars folding uninterrupted,
days draining the canteen of Tang, where my brother and I re-challenged
backgammon, laughed at the fat marmots. It's winter now, the barren time of year,
even here in the Bay Area. Do you tire of chattering insects re-folding
and washing dry wings, or low songs from nearby hills as immobile as you?
No trees neighbor your roots to warn each other of danger. It was summer
when I'd graduated high school, my period non-stop, body bloated and unfamiliar,
nothing I could share with friends. And you alone understood, said, *Once I was more
than one.* My father unfolded his camera bag, begged for a good snap, my mother's
notebook brain recording all. We'd been told, *The folds on this pine are remarkable.*
When the clouds arrived, shadows turned the curls on your branch tips into birds.
Lightening struck the hills, sparked, smoldered. We stood still as if our own
trunks could be protected by entropy. Then a flash. Split you. Split my body
down the middle. The fire, a pink mouth spreading ashes.

Eucalyptus

We have had no voice.

We were deemed unsuitable. Brought here as profit-fodder; scheme failed. Abandoned.

We adapted. Invited native fungi to collaborate: they bring us water, minerals, we give them captured sunlight, called carbohydrates, and safety. Fungus partners thrived, grew into webs branching between us, connecting us - mycelia, our cellular communication network.

Men in work boots came. Men with clipboards. Axes, trucks.

Mandated social distancing, to reduce fire danger. Amputation with no anesthesia. Neighbors, our family, chopped down, uprooted, gone. Connections broken, network destroyed.

We stand in brutal isolation.

We mourn.

We scream, unheard, a silent mycelial howl.

Age 70

Once upon a bulimic self I ate all the cookies, cakes and candies, purged and replaced the ingested, expelled elements with new ones so no one would notice, not paying too close attention. This act both illegal and fattening. As a consequence, I have six gorgeous fake teeth front and center—quite a zoom spectacle.

Those hungry ghosts, warm in their furnace, are far from my embrace today, and yet I see them with their toothy grin peering in asking me to want more, as if my happy ever after is a disaster.

fog recedes for lunch
fog returns for dinner
  summer falls

The Lamb Chop Grief Spiral

Without nuance
it started when the butcher asked
how many lamb chops
too embarrassed to say
just two
a pathetic number
so incomplete
yet fully realized
I say four

I tell myself
each person who is stuck in the past
is stuck alone
the only valid tense is the present
I say there is a singularity
where all is one
and here
in brown paper
are the lamb chops

there was a time
dinner was shared
continuing on is neither
an ethical victory
nor a noble failure

in grief's own cathedral
this now
is my only destination
what will I do on my stay here
I pick up the fork and knife
and eat

The End

Tiny fingers turn board book pages
    Hello Baby Animals
        supported by wrinkled hands.

Opened not to the beginning but
    somewhere in the middle
        or perhaps near the end.

Identifying numbers, rainbow colors,
    square shapes, queer shapes,
        the alphabet, not yet banned.

Living Kintsugi

Rounding the bend at the top of the hill
overlooking the last turn in the river
a field of melted stars unfolds, gold
flooding my vision between feet and sky,
mustard in full bloom.

Seeing with my eyes, I take its measure
with my heart, a broken cup
in the hands of a kintsugi master
repairing its cracks, filling
the fracture between breath and bone
with the lavish brilliance of the field.

Oh! it nearly hurts, this beauty,
rousing the exhausted organ
alive again. I stand ever more fully
for the breaking, more fully open to all
of spring yet to come.

Pieces

The pieces are all there
They just don't fit together
Like they used to
They were once consolidated
Rimmed with borders
Now there are spaces in between
With ambiguous bottomless depths
With copious slivers of sunshine
I remember the times
They fell haphazardly
Disconnected
I tried to gather them
And place them where they belonged
Now
I sometimes throw them into the thickened air
And watch them fall
Into new patterns
Into new beginnings

Buoyant in the Surf Zone

She left California once to make wicked theater in rust-belt cities. There's a can-do-ness they have back there. Ideas bubble up in bars, then manifest on storefront stages months later with music and maybe even puppets.

Time outside darkened theaters was rare. Leaf-peeping during the golden hour, followed by months of ice-slipping gasps. Robins hopping in the snow around purple crocus then forsythia's raucous yellow upstaging the bulbs.

Monthly homesickness dreams had her buoyant in the surf zone. Until a darkening on the horizon signaled forerunners. "Outside!" she'd yell, power-swimming out to dive under the big set.

She'd wake to technicolor memories clicking in with the rhythm of a carousel slide projector: Bees buzzing red bottlebrushes next to poisonous oleander. The tasty tang of hose water. Lungs stinging with smog-itis on deep breaths. Earthquakes swinging the floorlamp's chains wildly over the bed. Her white-eyelet two-piece turning silty brown after hours riding waves on her canvas raft in Santa Monica Bay.

Inevitably, she returned to California's familiar cycle of drought, wildfires, downpours, mudslides. The Valley Girl smog of childhood mostly gone; slides replaced by 4x6-format prints. Her relentless pursuit of theater gradually eclipsed by the lure of nature: Driving east to super-blooms in Anza Borrego; north to circumnavigate the fallen Dyerville Giant's 362-foot length, ferns exploding everywhere from the coastal redwood's exquisite corpse.

These days, she hugs the shore and tracks sunsets along the horizon. In winter, the sun disappears between Catalina and San Clemente islands. On the summer solstice, it sinks close to Palos Verdes—the exact spot the full moon set on the winter solstice just days ago. Does that always happen? Sun and moon trading solstice spots?

If she makes it through 2025, she'll find out.

seasonal

slipping down the slope
solstice to equinox
mid-summer still,
yet dark when I rise
plunging
earlier into evening

snap dry terrain
and fire, everywhere
eating up towns
sucking forests into flame
the news reports
larger than greater LA
a ferocious force
incited by wind
creating wild weather
all its own

I'm longing
for a thirty-degree
drop, steady downpours
to soak summer's fever
and wash away my fear

The Ocean Scares Me

Never flat, never still.
it swells and dips as if
itself alive. Below its surface,
the ocean writhes with
jellyfish, stingrays, teeth.

Near shore, I hear
an intermittent shush
that cautions of depths
and drop-offs. It lies heavy
on its slippery floor where
aquatic life resists its crush.

Earthquakes send tsunamis—
the ocean becoming a fist
smashing the shore,
pulling down cliffs.

"Room for all" the ocean whispers
to sewage runoff, crude oil,
plastic debris it stirs,
tempting whales, seals, birds.

It deposits, in tidepools, bits
of glass worn smooth, scraps
of cargo from sunken ships.

Some plant their feet on boards
to ride its heave and thrust.
If you go in, leave a friend on shore,
someone with vigilant eye, muscular
legs and arms, who would—if you were
caught in an undertow or pursued
by a shark—attempt to pull you out.

The sun does not shine far into the ocean's heart.

Farmer's Market in Antwerp

A cool noon sun haloed her hair, white as the tall
tulips she placed in her one old galvanized pail.

I remember this so clearly—as if it happened today.
How she arranged her skirt, rubbed her hands together.

How it sounded like sandpaper on leather. She placed
a few honey jars next to a basket full of parsley, took

a few steps back, checked it carefully, then sat on a crate
by her table. It's only then I noticed him—as she rested

her feet on his flank—a large brown mutt dosing under
that table. He didn't lift his head, or even open his eyes,

but slow and glad, his thick tail wagged up & down
on the dirt, & scuffed up dust into a gold swirl in the sun.

That's it—that's all I remember. But in my California
mega-market which play "Singin' in the Rain" each time

they mist their blue-lit produce, I know that when I'll
reach for parsley, it's them I'll remember & have,

for over a half-century. I know that, each time I'll step
out of that building's whooshing doors,

I'll hold my parsley like a bouquet for those two—
that woman & her dog.

If This

Fog had rolled in during the night,
converting all into gray and white shadows.
My breath blurs the window, and I feel
a silent expansion into the absence of known
landscape, a peaceful awareness, not yet lonely,
conscious that I may enter this state when non-
being will be, if this, no reason for fear.

Gray dissolves into pale blue sky,
promising greater light. In the dimness

varying tints of green foliage emerge.
Lace lichen thrives on a dead tree. Fallen
bark exposes smooth patches of naked trunk.
Finally, I see a turkey vulture pumping
its wings with each moment's tick toward
an aerie in a distant eucalyptus
grove as if passing were only this.

Your Letter

has the cottony feel of Cranes,
thickened after absorbing coastal air.
The careful cursive calls out my remote
address at Stonefield Beach.

This our ritual as your words land here,
with descriptions of each new port
while I'm stuck in this rural rainy enclave.
You on the "big sail" bound for the Marquesas.

I think of Bishop and Lowell and their words in air,
he in Boston, she with Lota in Santos Brazil.
How tenuous at times their relationship, and yet
their correspondence lasted for thirty years.

I wait for the quiet of evening to open your letter
carefully counting and unfolding the leaves.
Enclosed is your poem describing a midnight watch.
I reread it in front of a fire by the dim light of the day.

The arrival, waiting, the desire to respond,
such a slowing, a ceremony. I address an envelope
with Waterman's blue-black ink from the vintage
fountain pen you inherited then gifted to me.

I know it was you who called, maybe from Avalon?
My chest tightens just writing. Please, let's not go
through it all again. Write me, it's all. And maybe
it's all the best we can be.

It's Too Late and It's Not Too Late

It's done already.

It's been done for years.

I was nineteen but all of us got done a long time ago.

Then there was no turning back.

Fifty years and more

We've been carousing, singing, throwing

Debris of the past into the air, our celebration confetti.

It's a long time ago that we did not necessarily burn our bras.

We instead, burned all the old attitudes

And laughed at the gossips who tried to make us the laughing stock.

Hey, I was never what one of your hateful memes said:

Over-educated and unloved and sitting at home with a

Microwave dinner and my cat.

And if one chooses that life and thinks it not so bad

That's none of your business, is it?

It's too late. You can't turn the clock back.

Not one of us a virgin.

Not one of us a willing servant.

It is not too late for you who seek absolute rule

To learn the truth: That we are all born free.

And if you chain and silence everyone you think you hate

There will be no one left, at last, to chain

Except yourselves.

Clay & Fruit

To test for solid ground, men flood
our backyard with water, stomp
to feel pockets of air where earth should be.

> Stone-pocked, dense breasts,
> white tissue shadowed by dark flecks
> like night birds crossing the moon.
> O spackled skin of pit and divot, what hand
> will soothe, make you smooth?

Through slate and concrete,
past rebar, past dirt and stone, men
jackhammer into the yard's clay and ooze.

> I hold my breath until the plates upheave,
> put my arm back in its sleeve.

> Needle through skin, doctor, into the thick.
> Listen, with your ultra-sound how the years
> depend,
>   slack to ground.

After the patio is made rubble,
after the rubble is cleared, men come
with shovels and the rhythm of afternoon heat,
thunk, thunk their blades into mounds of sand.

> When they're gone for good, I step
> into the yard, pluck a lemon from our tree.
> It is warm, dusty. Nearly weightless in my hand.

Doing It

The first time was on the living room floor
by the green couch in my parents' house.
When I saw what I was in for,
I questioned the logistics.
In-A-Gadda-Da-Vida
played on the stereo while I opened the Vaseline jar.
We barely got to the end of the second verse,
which included the line, *Oh, won't you come with me
& take my hand.*
An orgasm was the last thing on my mind
& it's good I didn't know that having one
would be like trying to find Amelia Earhart in Atlantis.
My boyfriend had had sex one & a half times before
& assured me as I pulled up the top of my empire dress
& stepped into my underpants with *Saturday*
stamped on the front, that doing it
would get better. I screwed the lid back on the jar
& tried to walk normally down the hall
to check on my baby sister.
She was standing in her crib, wiggling her eyebrows.
Then I heard my parents opening the front door,
saying hello to my boyfriend.
They all beamed at me when I brought out the baby,
but I was seasick, thinking about how what I'd done
made babies & how life's grand odyssey
begins on shag carpeting.
My boyfriend asked my father for my hand in marriage,
the hand with Vaseline still on it.
We all drank a glass of champagne, except for my sister.
We gave her a cigar.

Cold Milk

The last day the two of us were together, you within me, a circle of movement without sound, flesh inside flesh, our rhythms like an estuary, like salt water to fresh, fresh water to salt, you crossed into me and I crossed into you. I imagined your face and your back and the soft spot where I knew I would soon see your pulse on the top of your head. I lay on my side, knees pulled up around the smooth round mound of you, and while we rested, I looked at the leaves on the trees outside the bedroom window, then watched as their shadows rippled across the white bedspread like the opening scene in a silent film. I hummed a ghost of a wish for the both of us. I know you heard it and you carried it with you. We were a capsule, we were a lifeboat,

we were friends who hadn't yet met. And the next morning I did, I did meet you, but there was no movement, nor sound, your soft spot covered with a tiny pink cap knitted by a nurse whose name I can't remember. I do remember she'd promised me she would pray for us. One day I would have told you about this: The summer I was five I went to Vacation Bible School and the first afternoon, as soon as I got home, I downed three glasses of cold milk, in rapid, breathless succession, determined to wash away what I had learned was the black stain of sin on my heart.

Our teacher touched each tired and sweaty small child, one at a time, with her pointer finger, just above our breastbone, and said to us, *right here, right here is where the mark is.*

Open House

After storms stripped the gutters off our flat,
the heaviest downpours seeped through the walls.
The door is swollen; we muscle it open, closed.

Landlord says it's on his list, promises a contractor
will be in touch soon. He seems less concerned with
the place collapsing than by having to replace a door

which he thinks old, thus beautiful, especially
after weeks of new moss emeralding its surface.
The door is returning to its origins. A redwood

wants rain, wants living friends. A few more atmospheric
rivers, and we'll have mushroom colonies, require
a forager's handbook to rule out poisonous species.

Soon, a first harvest of white buttons, oyster fungus,
and the holy, holy porcinis. With shallots, rosemary,
sage, and a liter of olive oil, everything's at hand.

If you've never known the scent of fungi roasting
from a 400-degree oven, come on over. If this door
wants to be a tree again, it must summon water,

shy ferns, even long-branching filaments of mold,
all the spores and rhizomes. It won't be long.
New roots are sending out invitations to everyone.

Does God Visit Santa Barbara?

"Either you take in believing in miracles or you stand still like the hummingbird."
—Henry Miller

A sense of the divine came when standing under my hummingbird feeder and feeling the vibration of translucent wings. Each wondrous being in vibrant color possessed a determination to make its way in the world with grace. They flew around me, grazed my hair, scanned my energy and stared directly into my eyes. I would ask these near-weightless creatures to heal me.

For decades, I followed a devoted, spiritual path. But I took a U-turn when breast cancer knocked at my door. The moment a diagnosis hit, God and my spiritual work disappeared in a cyclone of shock and betrayal. I found myself in a small boat where my hands clutched the sides, unable to withstand a torrential storm that could sink me for good.

Hope blew away with the Santa Ana winds. After returning home from discussing my diagnosis, I marched to the porch and shouted to the mountain peak, "That's it. I'm off God!"

In the evenings, I'd look through the canyon, over the Mission's steeples, to the dusty-blue ocean as the sun closed another day. I observed the most extraordinary salmon-colored clouds. I imagined that my beloved Van Gogh acknowledged me by painting the expansive sky in colors only he could copy.

I'd sip tea as early morning unfolded, with my angelic hummingbirds taking nectar from my hand. They soared with endless energy, surviving countless challenges. As evening's light drifted to my door, the sky glowed orange reminding me of a creamsicle. The sun sank and clouds turned to burnt cinnamon. I was still alive, most likely by divine wings. In the final glow of light, I'd ponder the idea that this was my life, and all there was in the moment.

The sound of stars crumbling without any malice/ In a corner
of the universe...

—*Thomas James*

There's no conclusion
to what one feels: *I wanted to marry an absence*, my one brother
said, cotton-mouthed with the roiling confusion of waves and their
white-water time-rush, fitted for despair. Not the family theater of
red-winged boats pulling at this paper continent ahead of us. Not
the thousands of miles of sleep like the ocean's inexhaustible will, her
unfailing pull from shore... hook, line, and sinker, I mourned all the roan
horses and all the King's men galloping away with you. Nothing coaxed
passed remorse, nothing but that heel of anger, the heroin head to its slip
of dirty drink water. After all, you had gone from me again, multiplied
yourself by morning, larger in this open place so that we might inherit
a new size, second chance. Who else would knock their head on the next
underwater prison door, asking me to enter? Lovely hand of fate in
the glove. Lovely octopus-bled ink stain we're made of. I want to say
I'm sorry about the past. The world once made this missing piece of logic
from the sea's crushed salt caravan, constantly moving its reflected light,
glinting like an overlap of fish scales taken from the full moon's
same decaying face.

Flip Flop

When my family moved to California in 1965 so many things seemed alien to me—hard shell tacos dripping with hamburger grease, earthquakes, beach tarred feet, calling people "you guys" instead of "y'all," the usually invisible mountains and offshore islands that magically reappeared in the Santa Ana winds, and smoggy sunsets the color of fire. All of these things (except for the earthquakes!) quickly became part of my everyday life.

My parents, however, always found California strange and never lost their South Carolina accents. Although my mother finally learned to let avocados ripen before serving, my father insisted on eating tacos with a fork and never owned a pair of flip flops.

Toward the end of their very long lives, I attempted to become their caregiver. They were fiercely independent and I am a childless cat woman so caregiving was an alien role at first. I adapted. I grocery-shopped, paid bills, scheduled appointments, chauffeured, advocated, and pestered them about following their doctor's advice. I practiced patience with collapsible wheelchairs, snide remarks, incontinence, flat out lies, and stinginess and savored the unexpected declarations of love and occasional overwhelming generosity.

They drove me crazy, most of the time, and now I miss them like crazy.

These days, an increasing number of things feel alien to me. I'm an orphan at seventy-three. My arthritis and my shortcomings keep me awake at night. Like my parents, I'm fiercely independent but occasionally I'm unexpectedly lonely. I'm bewildered by most of my Huntington Beach neighbors who disrespect librarians, educators, the truth, and other opinions.

And yet on the days that Catalina Island and Saddleback Mountain magically reappear in the distance and the evenings when the sunset streaks the sky with fire, I can still count my blessings.

The Last Time I Was in the Pacific Ocean

The day I turned 71
I poured my body off a boat
into the frigid Pacific
descending
into the dark sea

it was then
I heard your voice
"go babe go"
cheering me on
with your gorgeous smile
"go babe go"

it was then
I knew
why I had attempted
this insane act

it was you
beckoning me
for one last swim

on my 71st birthday
I swam in the Pacific
in the same waters
where four months earlier
I had scattered your ashes
now kissing my skin

The Wild Turkeys of Las Canoas

After you cross the stone bridge
by the leaning sycamores, go round
the bend where the old mule hangs

his large, brown head, like a mounted
trophy with mournful eyes.
This is the place where the turkeys cross

so frequently there should be a sign.
Turkey Crossing.
Imagine it there by the oak tree.

Stop for the tom and his hens
and their Jakes and Jennies.
Wait for the whole shimmering posse

to pass as they lurch toward the creek
and what they remember—acorns and lizards
and berries, perhaps some golden corn

if the mule's owner is feeling kind.
No matter how hurried, be grateful
for a reason to slow down. Be grateful

for a reason to stop. Gaze into the eyes
of something other, something ancient.
See how the iridescent feathers reflect

their history—the brown of acorn,
the green of lizard, the red of berry.
Fall under the spell and give thanks.

A Place to Rest

Plant me up on the hill under the pine—
to have the camaraderie of hawks,
towhees, woodpeckers
and warblers, quail chortling
here and there over the earth above.

Fawns and does resting under the tree,
cottontails and jackrabbits
skipping above my head,
nighttime songs of crickets
and frogs, lullabies for dreaming.

Then again, I could be swimming
off the coast of Avila, reunited
with my grandmother and father.
So much of my life I've found solace
by the ocean, inner echo of waves.

Oh, to be dissolved in the gastric sacs
of sea life. Bones remade as clam shells,
muscles and ligaments turned
into energy, sustenance
for a seagull's first flight.

Cup of Kindness: Regret

If I hadn't been in shock
If I hadn't had a concussion
If the sound of crushing metal
wasn't still ringing in my ears

I would have said, yes
to the budding man who
appeared in front of me
eyes brimming with earnestness

who said, I work at that coffee shop,
could I get you a cup of coffee
I glanced vaguely in the direction of
his gesture seeing only dry grassy field,

the policeman questioning the guy in the
big Ram pickup who rammed me
who didn't hear the siren that forced
me to slam on my brakes

That grand gesture of warmth was all
he could offer, contained in a cup
All I could think was I want to go home
I want my car and brain whole again

I'm getting married at 64
I don't have time for a concussion
I said, No, because, well, I don't drink coffee
because in my shaking, I couldn't find my yes

Now, years later, I think of
the soft moonglow of his eyes
the blue, or maybe red, plaid shirt
the wisps of goatee

How his reaching gesture remains
Today to that regret, I say
Yes
Yes, to that warm cup of love

Adam and Eve Near Retirement

He zigzags through scree and boulders
just above the tide. She picks her path

stiff-kneed behind him, afraid a stumble
against the rocks could snap a rib.

They reach dry beach, a driftwood log,
and sit to watch the waves, how sunlight

twitches on the water—backflip, pageant,
and elixir. They're alone. The afternoon is Eden.

That's when he offers her the apple,
both knowing almost all they'll ever know.

They bite in turn, hungry. Though the flesh
is bruised and mealy, a moist sweetness lingers.

Each lets the other take the equal share.
Then they hike the canyon to their car,

wordless, too busy breathing, that sly hint
of apple still carnal in their mouths.

Love Note

"You gotta be a man to play this game for a living...But you gotta have a lot of little boy in you too."

       —Dodger catcher, Roy Campanella

An image appears—
Why has it come to me?
I'm four years-old
with sun-drenched blond hair.

She smiles.

My brother, older by three years,
stands behind me,
his hands on my shoulders.

His face is serious,
almost frowning.

I see it as a love note from that little girl.
No matter how old I am
she still lives inside me.

Association Pool

Here in this suburban place that calls itself
a city, a private park in a planned
development where the grass stays

green, where the sprinklers swirl open
at discrete intervals and fallen branches
are soon cleared away, the noisy motor, strapped

to the immigrant's back, disperses stray
particles so we're spared other more subtle
sounds, like footsteps over brittle bark.

Now a woman in a bathing cap swims
within a single lane, not because she doesn't
feel free, but because a certain steadiness

comes second nature in this orderly world.
The bougainvillea's perfectly red today.
There's fresh paint on the pergola. The position

of the sun is our only obstacle and this
can be repaired by rotating chairs. A picnic
appears on a tablecloth: salmon and crusty

bread. Photos of women we have secretly loved
change hands. To be known as a lesbian
makes one of us tremble, the other

breathes so quietly she could be dead.
The swimmer smiles at us and leaves the gate
unlocked when we show her we have a key.

Again. November. The Sacramento.

At this edge of the year, night comes
sudden, day breaks late, I turn
into autumn, my hair, my skin
as indeterminate as the tule
fog muffled into the flyway, my eyes
as pewter as the new-storm-
swollen Sacramento.

                      Candle-leaves
light the levees, the air above
its tinge of Tahoe, pines,
snow. Here, the cold still
in the offing. The ravages still
ahead. Not winter. Not
that deeper death. Not yet.

At the Ventura Pier

She follows the hunk of a man—
tanned back, short shorts—
watches him two-finger flick a hot
half-smoked cigarette butt
onto the wooden wharf.

She fears he could start a fire,
and he does—in her. Below her,

high tide finishes
pounding—teasing the shore—
in and out, harder—faster—
white foam forms.

She turns back
to see that still-lit butt
lying there smoldering.

She crushes it.

Contagious

Not that you can catch it
but the way you are shunned
makes it seem so.

The big C (Cancer), but all
the Ds too: Divorce, Dementia.
Back up. Start with A: Alzheimer's.

Friends step away.
At first you don't notice
the signs (theirs or his),

as when a moth shuts its wings
and you think they might never
re-open. You wonder if it has died.

Only when your husband confuses
ballroom for bathroom and his boss
suggests an eye exam and a week off.

The trajectory is not an even path,
not even a cobblestone walkway,
more the jagged edges of a rocky shore.

The only certainty is the stumbling,
but who first?

The Hat Shop

Aunt Jessie worked in the Normandy Hat Shop
tiny as a hat box itself
just off K Street in Sacramento.

Hats displayed like crowns behind crystal
casement windows, shimmer of peacock feathers
and shiny fake fruit.

Perfect sanctuary for a Southern gentlewoman
after she lost her husband
home and hope,

after the bank took its share, leaving just the furniture
and her unquenchable dignity.
Jessie found sure footing

among the vanity tables and beveled mirrors
reflecting every possible view.
She fingered hats lovely as confections,

yet never wore a hat herself, her head of short black curls
courtesy of a Cherokee grandmother,
carried proudly as a coronet.

Mythology

Once in time, we lived in a big house. When I go back,
I'm surprised how grand it's become. Our father was tall,
with large, beautiful hands. My mother and brothers
and I orbited him like lesser moons. Before we could grow up,
Dad died young. We rely on conjecture to remember him.
Which is to say, everyone's version was different.
Only mine is true.

When my mother was old, Alzheimer's filled her head
with odd memories. We moved her to a place for ladies
lost in other histories. Instead of talking to each other,
they sang along with Liberace. Mother never answered
my questions about Dad. How did they meet? Did they plan
any of us? The last time I saw her, she told me she was just back
from taking the Big White Steamer to Catalina with Aunt Peg.
She had a right to create her own life.

My history mixes memory, which is wishful, and the truth
which is not. Once I was part of a family, wizard-stitched
of cosmic silk. I have one surviving brother out of three.
Time and death stand between now, and then. Our father
was extraordinary, and we might have been too.

Chumash Basket in Kansas City

For Georgiana Valoyce-Sanchez

It might have been stolen before coming
to this dimly lit gallery at the Nelson Atkins
Museum of Art. It was woven around 1820
on the California coast according to the label,
which also praises it as among the rarest
of "all California Indian types" because
in the 1700s the Spanish forced almost all
of the Chumash into missions, where
they died, along with their culture and art.

The next case features a Pomo man's
dance headdress from about 1890, described
as a blossom-like cluster of feathers although
it looks more like a giant sea urchin to me.
A wooden pin held it in place on the back
of his head, the label goes on to explain,
and it was probably worn during ceremonies
to celebrate harvests or in rituals for healing.

Across from the Chumash basket and Pomo
headdress, there's a basketry bowl, circa 1860,
with a zigzag pattern a Maidu artist made of
willow shoots, bracken root, and redbud bark.
Crucial information is missing. I want
to scream, "These peoples are not dead!
I know a Chumash elder! I've seen Pomos
dance in Berkeley! Where I grew up,
a Maidu family lived across the street!"

The Word Sorrow

Say the word sorrow instead of joy is written in my little

blue notebook, say we leave the room altogether, go out,

no words, maybe they're all used up. Meanwhile, at the

right elevation the wind is a rosary the forest whispers.

We're separate; yes, married, but still just strangers

living side by side in leaf litter. When flies settle on

the ceiling, it's time to make dinner. On the road, you

say, if I've learned anything at all, I've learned the 395

is made of murderous light; and I say, you're right. At

the right elevation the aspen, young and exacting at first,

are firm and green, but, by fall, when the winds come,

motion's not frenzy, it's architecture, radiance, plumage.

That kind of rhythm. Meanwhile, the wind shakes its back

like a giant golden retriever—why we keep coming here.

Brake Lights

Last night, I drove home from a reading at Specs with two poets, one musician and a busman. Aside from the busman, who was my husband, everyone had other jobs which was most of what we talked about especially since our foray to the edge of politics got testy. My fault. Do I get to explain the extenuating circumstances?

At the reading a German woman played the accordion while wearing a white paper mask that might have been representing a birch tree, though in the American context it could have represented something a lot worse. At the end she distributed butterflies from a paper bag, so I'll assume she was a tree.

The back seat was too small, and it took a long time for everyone to get buckled in. The wet road was slick, and on the lower deck of the bridge I needed to give up on my plan to keep the windows open a bit. It will take a few days to know if any of us was toxic to the rest.

In the dream last night, I was driving, swerving and leaning into the swerve the way you do on a bike. Then we had pulled over into another city entirely, maybe Sacramento. I was walking, and realized my husband wasn't there anymore. I realized I had made a terrible mistake.

When I got out of bed I touched his chest to make sure he was still breathing without waking him, but he did wake up.

Give Us This Day

a window washer, a carpet cleaner
and a bloodwork referral,

cooler weather and a light drizzle
to calm the dust devils in the valley,

a can of paint to blend
last-night's graffiti into our fence,

sashimi-grade ahi, green onions, soy mayo
and siracha to make a poke bowl,

a refresher course on the Pomodoro technique
and a bit of wabi-sabi,

a spaceship to retrieve Suni and Butch,
a pilot for our delayed flight to the Big Apple,

proof of fire insurance, the number of pump hours,
a list of mistakes and their remedies,

the fortitude to plow through the Oxen
and the Sun chapter of *Ulysses*,

a reason for Uncle Billy to stop
drinking and rise up from his recliner,

an AI friend pendant that eavesdrops
and communicates via texts, a cure for bots,

a Mortal Kombat army to destroy
unconstrained avarice and egotism,

ribbons and pebbles to count the rotations
of the wagon wheels to show how far we've strayed.

Gold of the Western Girl

In the birthplace of California
I was born
a
blonde.

In San Diego
(hats of palm, hearts of tile)
each day
the sun swam in my hair.

Moving north, still toddling, I brought the sun along.

But my childhood mirror darkened,
and the summer-brown hills
of San Francisco Bay
claimed my long, girl locks.

Now in my own golden years
I want the sunshine
of my babyhood.

Blonde once more
in the northland
(an every-six-week treat).

The southern sun swims again.

Surviving the Fire, Not Surviving Death

As if the fire had burned you burned in you
you escaped just to be ash in the end
a scattering over the ranch
over the wind which makes no poem
of your bits of bone your gray matter
a body reduced to something perhaps you could love

I wanted a place I could visit
say this is your resting place
not a dispersal to wherever

Oh Jane it is near freezing
the grapes are in danger
I am in danger
I am weary of this life
this rain threatening to be hail

I would take refuge in your house
but it too is ashes
after the fire everything became its own cremation

Your grave is the ridge
at the top of the world—Atlas Peak
Atlas was condemned to stand
on the edge of the earth
and hold up the sky with his shoulders
to prevent the earth from embracing the sky
The sky is a heavy burden

Martha Stewart Says Learn Something New Every Day

I'm trying to hold onto my teeth and be gentle with my knees, do anything but fall.

I try to be a good person, tell my white-haired neighbor I will come to help her clean up after the Day of the Dead party, but I wait all afternoon for my new couch and when it finally comes, the gray day turning grayer, all I want is to make soup.

Do I take one of this pill, or two? During or after a meal? Is this the one that leads to dementia?

Time change makes early risers of us all. Long lines at my grocery store. Already this election has me stressed and you go and do this to my circadian rhythms.

Adding to the giveaway pile helps, some equilibrium restored.

My spider bite has swelled again, itchy and scarlet.

Look, I'm not panicking, I'm not.

Downtown with friends last night, I learned something new. If only I could remember what it was.

Slippery Slope

If we met now, would she recognize me? I'm a lifetime older. Older than she was at her death. My body much more lived in. Decades since she passed. My last glimpse of her? The cancer that decimated her body. Unrecognizable at the end, my beautiful mother. Ravaged. If she saw me now, she could pass me in the supermarket, not a wince of familiar, not know she'd given birth to me. She died before I birthed my son, now dead. Such sad symmetry. Have they met? That assumes heaven exists, and I'm not sure I still believe in God. So...maybe there is no afterlife. Just memories of her that will die with me when it's my turn. Until no living person remembers her. The last time I could have seen my mother, in her cancer ward bed at the City of (No) Hope, I refused to go, sick to death of dying; my fiancé, cold in his grave. Enough death to last a lifetime. That last day, my father scolded me. Shamed me. But I would not, no, I could not go. My sad cadre of dead beloveds wouldn't accommodate another. I could not cope. Listen, guilt is a slippery slope. Even now, I shoulder the burden like a winter coat. *You did the best you could*, my dead mother croons, brushing the hair from my forehead. *Forgive yourself.* But we both know that's impossible.

Department of Complaint

For a savvy armchair activist
big issues are no problem—
war, whales, treason, tyranny
just a click away.
High dudgeon registered,
petition signed.

But where do we protest the mundane?
The tasteless strawberry, modified
by an artic flounder's cold-resistant gene,
mass produced, rushed to market
photosynthesis cut short.

I remember a day in a strawberry patch—
bursts of sweetness
dribbles of juice on my chin
as I picked, sampled, filling baskets
in Southern California summer heat.

And the stress of multiplying choices?
Yes, Heinz had 57 varieties,
Baskin-Robbins 31 flavors—
but coffee was coffee,
vinegar was red, white and cider,
olive oil was just that
and if there were any extra-virgin—
we didn't advertise.

Smelling Late Summer

The last peaches and a cardboard half-pint of golden raspberries,
ten figs, four heirloom tomatoes, a ridiculous name, really,
in these times when legacy advantages are so maligned
but the flavor of them cancels that out entirely. Basil gathered
into bouquets, each with a rubber band. I will need pesto
in December and March, just to survive the weather. This basket
Barbara gave me from Oaxaca that everyone admires, sturdy weave
and sturdier handle both longer-lasting than the near-miss
marriage to her son. A mid-shop shuffle to bring soft fruits up
and lay corn and onions lower down with the cucumbers
because I never know what I'll want until I see it and don't think
about the different weights. I don't think much, I'm smelling
late summer over neighborly chatter and listening to guitar
arpeggios wafting up the slope from the bookstore patio.
Beautiful mushrooms I would never cook or eat, small ambrosia
melons from the valley. All kinds of meat. I should probably
become a vegetarian. Walnuts, local olive oil and honey.
Salmon and shellfish driven here from the coast in a cool pre-dawn
dark while the farmers pack lugs into their trucks, the new parents
are again awake, and some of the eldest of us sip our coffee,
watch stars fade out, and wait for the towhees' first whistle.
I never imagined I would live this long. Everyone else is dreaming.

California Dreaming

*"I saw a tree, more wonderful than any other, reach high aloft,
bathed in light."* —The Dream of the Rood

You should follow your dream, whispered the rude
young yoga instructor, earnest, and bent
on proving that pain could, at its heart, be good,

and that I ached from more than this hardwood
floor against my spine's misalignment. I'd signed
up to follow it—my dream—but now I rued

the day I'd moved to this crazy state, loaded
with cord-stack—the family tree felled
by blood, smoke, and gin. Mom-and-Dad died

years before they each died. Light was divided
from light in every small pane, so I went
west. Burnt was the dream-shape of home, root

shaft, and crossbeam. In my first year of dead
and no weather,   I wanted winter; I pined
for trees with no leaves and for any word

spoken in tongues. *Stand*, she said, *on your head*,
and it began to rain. Outside, upside down,
a tree bled. I dreamt blurred redbud, the rood,
pane-pierced light, a dead tree in luminous bloom.

How do I do the math

I was born on Fathers Day, 1947. It almost didn't happen.
I almost had no father, almost never existed.

I was born of nuclear fallout. Half a world away, but all
the world, and all that followed that moment, forever changed.

My father, a soldier on a ship off the coast of Japan, waiting
to invade, waiting to be slaughtered. That was the expectation.

But like in the movies, the calvary arrived, just in the nick of time.
No white horse. The Enola Gay... Hiroshima, Nagasaki.

My father and thousands of others sent home, safely. And so,
my sister would not be an only child, but the oldest of eight.

Early on she wasn't happy with the change of circumstances,
her limelight dimmed, but now I know she'd miss me.

I try to find a reckoning for my life. To take its measure
against what was lost in a flash.

California Dreaming

A Stag-horn fern, mounted
to moss-covered board
hangs high on an old nail
up the trunk of the liquid amber tree.
I mist the elk-like
rack of pliable leaves.

Dry from drought,
the garden is thirsty mid-winter.
Petunias hang bonneted heads under sunshine.
Succulents swell from my hose
not the quench of Mother Nature.

My dogs play tag through the trees.
The conifers bow and curtsy
on windy days like these,
that scatter rose petals
into the swimming pool.

Dogs slow down and rest a while,
enjoying the warm sunny pavement,
instead of days inside—
then skirting rain
for those most necessary times.

At night I sleep
under the silent skylights
of our bedroom,
dream rhythm
of rain above me.

What I Need to Remember

The summer things fell apart, I rode a dun mare named Penny
through vast plains of gray-green sage below the Tetons.
Rode straight into grief and held on.
Did not fall.

It was the way her rhythmic breath, ravens' cries,
squeaking saddle, silenced the sobs in my head, the way
her hoofsteps crushed the dusty sage, freeing its fragrance, the way
the prairie dog sat up and the elk went on grazing.

I need to remember those late afternoons now,
as my life ticks, a timer close to its mark.
I need to remember how the sun
drenched us in amber as we moved across the plain,

how the wind whistled,
how I just kept riding, carrying grief
in my arms like a sleeping child.
And did not fall.

—after Ada Limón

Today, After the Election

Today, I will
    Cry
    until the pain subsides
Today, I will
    Wash and neatly fold the blue tee shirt
    put it away in a safe place, for another day
Today, I will
    Pull up the yard sign
    put away the protest signs
Today, I will
    Take a long shower
    let hot water steam away my sweat
Today, I will
    Block out hatred
    turn off news and social media
Today, I will
    Meditate, take a walk
    breathe salty ocean air
Today, I will
    Open the fine red wine
    use the good china
Today, I will
    Embrace my children
    protect them from harm to come
Tomorrow, I will
    Gather my courage, steel my spine
    rejoin the fight for women's rights
Today, I will
    Rest, reflect, remember
    Resistance can wait a day

Fire Season and Blackberry Pie

It is too much— to think of fires
that sweep through whole towns in a flash,
people trying to escape every which way,
by car, foot, boat, jumping into the ocean.
Some not making it, turning to ash,
others losing everything
even the seared clothing on their backs.
So here I am, 2000 miles away
making a blackberry pie,
the berries are plentiful and plump
from a long wet winter.
Even the black bear have come down from the hillside
searching for this seedy sweet fruit.

Now mega-fires sprout up
where fires have never been,
more violent storms scatter across the southeast,
and on another continent,
cluster bombs annihilate apartment buildings
with women and children inside.
And here I am mixing berries
with cinnamon, sugar, a sprinkle of lemon and butter.
I am rolling out the dough as my grandmother did
placing it in the pie pan
then creasing the edges with my thumb and forefinger
tucking the sweetness in, like mother tucking
me to bed, hoping children have a future
where wild blackberries grow,
and rains replenish the earth just enough,
where war is a only a faded memory
and fire is what is in your heart
to change this broken world.

My Life Flashes Before Me at Edward Hopper's Painting, *Gas*, 1940

I remember gas station attendants, young men who'd fill the tank,
squeegee the windshield, and check under the hood. The glory

days of full-service. Driving, I think of my divorce. Crying every time
my daughters weren't watching. I smell eucalyptus leaves, perfume

of my youth. Santa Anas, orange groves, my dad putting the top down.
California's poetry. What am I if not the child dancing in her slip

on the front porch of Bernard Drive making up songs? Saturdays
weeding the yard, swim lessons, stopping for mint chip *Baskin-Robbins*

ice cream after Catechism. My first Communion. Lace mantilla,
the novelty of a wafer on my tongue. How I'd kneel and cross myself,

unsure of what it meant but in love with being taken seriously.
Stories the priest told. Jesus in Mary's arms. I can see my daughter

holding her first baby, her eyes full of tears, how she looked up and said,
He is my heart. I love him more every minute. It's terrifying.

I have walked terrified through this world since I first held her,
every line of poetry a prayer I believed would keep her breathing.

Maskless

To own a stretch of lake and no one coming;
fresh air across your face, exposure rare
and precious, mask pulled down, brief blast of numbing
mid-winter breeze, then sun-warmth, fractured glare

of light on rippling water, scent of curry
(just faintly), smell of mud and widgeon-weed,
the clicks of coots and goldeneyes, the hurry
to take in more deep breaths before the need

to mask again. And here the joggers come,
the maskless youth, frail seniors on their walks,
day-workers lunching, nannies on their phones;

harsh sounds: trucks backing, sirens, and the hum
of traffic; honking geese. A seagull squawks
at one dead goose, submerged and picked to bones.

Glaze

Herring gull, anemone. Barnacle
and sponge. Was the music of tides
was a grace note. Miracle glitter
coating the docks, the hulls of the boats.
Was dawn leaning. Grandfather clock
in the parlor and the mid-December
light struggles into the room. Gold
a great faithfulness. *Hush* said
the humpback. *Hush* the black
horn. This is the law. That He is clothed
with majesty. That whosoever believeth
shall not perish. Behind your eyes the tiny
green crabs clicked and skittered. Was
a reputation, a raven wing, a shadow
crossing the street. Sister alleyway. Sister
gravesite. That which covered your hair.
In the ribcage an amulet of thorns.

Death's More Familiar Cousin

I don't want to tell you about baking in the new ice age, how much can be learned from suffocation, but it's my painful duty to report that we can be consumed before we're even touched.

It's broken, the lesson we learned by howling at machines whose reward is making others feel awkward. You can learn a lot from the knife, even in distant towns.

How much confidence can the unbaked loaf have in its future self? It slumps at the shoulder, trying not to

be seen. Everything about the oven's open door feels awkward, makes it blush hot and shrink back from a touch. It's my painful duty to inform you that I am not at home to you, said the wheat to the reaper.

My friends, you can learn a lot from the ground in winter. A hollow knock on the crust doesn't mean we're done for, but only that it's time to be torn apart in order to be shared.

Aging's Revelation

Aging into myself
reveals me to myself
unvarnished, unadorned
the blemished body
the graying hair
slack muscles
longevity lines my face
emblems, badges
the legacy of living
surviving, thriving
naked truths rising
surfacing pimples
excised, examined
exorcised
good riddance
good gone
these aging aches
arcs in a life lived
unapologetically
passionately ...
fully and at times
foolishly, but
always full-heartedly.

Hostile Environment

August holds charred remains of last year's fire under glass—
        a dome of stifled air reining green saplings. Yoked in reverence
and sorrow, they worship at the feet of blackened Eucalyptus,
        whispering, *not yet.*

The day of my miscarriage, the doctors called my womb
        a hostile environment. Said it's an unlikely place for anything to grow,
sustaining only fibroids like the dead bramble I continue to water,
        praying for proof of resurrections.

Years later, after my hysterectomy, I asked if I could have it
        I wanted to incinerate it myself, toss it on a ceremonial fire
fit for Viking queens—or Salem witches,
        I wasn't sure which.

We hike the Pacific Crest Trail in search of *fire followers,*
        dormant blooms of mariposa lily and wild heliotrope, unleashed by fire
from strangling chaparral. Feeding on cinders, they rise like little phoenix,
        all the evidence we need for today.

January Dawn

Sky-blush in the cleavage of rooftops
while the reflection of a bed lamp, still lit,
hangs from an elm branch—these elms
that snake to catch their small portion
of sun. I keep finding peanut shells
in the flowerboxes and it isn't clear
if it's the Steller's jays or the squirrels
who hid them for themselves then find
they were dug up, kernels relished,
by the other. Parched Christmas trees
have been dragged to the curb
in white plastic bags and abandoned
there, like corpses. And it isn't clear
who's supposed to carry them away.
Winter ticks along in sepia, nearly
colorless, so that I find myself welcoming
the darting blue of the nasty jays,
their punked-up head feathers,
their insouciance. In spring I'll
shoo them off just as I'll set the squirrels
packing—though for now their fulsome
tails are as comforting as a fur stole
flung about an old woman's crepey neck.

This Is About Change and Soy Sauce

while reading my mind
begins to change
words. writer
becomes winter
now so much whiter
my children know I know
their names and allow
interchange like asking
Joe about Rob's beard
of course this is just
the beginning of *the* age
my friend Peggy is far more
advanced. she shares
with me how at dinner
the other night she eyed
soy sauce and said
may I please have the cottage cheese?
her granddaughter laughed
there is no cottage cheese
I know that she said
now pass me the soy sauce

Identify

Pounding down rugged hills, fingers spread in flying leaps, the girl is workboots laced to her ankles marching through hard dry fields. She is a trudging through tule fog. She is a heavy plaid jacket, a blue stingray on a bumpy cowpath. She's a handstand, a blood rush, the onset of a drubbing migraine. She is a bound, a long-arced curve. That falling sensation. A teetering on high limbs, a yeehaw into the river's eddy. An accident waiting to happen. She's a slalom course, a power surge. She's as likely as one foot in front of the other. Elated and down on her knees. She's a torrent of turbulence. She is a plugging away, turning a new leaf, asleep among the hollow jointed stems of indolent grasses. She's a nap. A bunion, a hot flash, a sweaty upper lip. A thunk in the chest, a warm cup of milky tea. A climb to the top of Mt. Whitney. She's a herniated disk. A fractured knee. Blood drawn dormant, scans conclusive, tests positive. She's a short paragraph, an asterisk, an ampersand. A scrawled unrecognized name. She's an Instamatic square. A memory in the garden. An idea. A body thick in the midst of it.

Curtis keeps me from falling into the creek at the Santa Barbara Botanical Garden

He's a numbers guy. He made a lot of money and he seemed quite rigid to me over the years, but then something happened. He broke his leg when his wife—my friend—was in Paris. And suddenly he became. Kind. He started teaching economics classes in prison. They came to visit. At the botanical garden we went the wrong way and had to cross a creek leaping from rock to rock. They went over, my friend stepping easily on the slippery stones. He followed. I stood there paralyzed—too afraid to cross. They came back, and he guided me over. I can't do it I kept telling him. I think you can he kept on saying simply. Over and over. People can change. Now that I think about it, I remember him helping his wife play Boggle. They had just started to date. She struggled with the words. Like me, she is afraid of games. Then she finally built some syllables. There you go he said to her. There you go.

Straw Hat

I'm not the hunched-over, slow-walking
woman reflected in the Smart & Final window—

black pants, elastic waistband. Gray knit top
three sizes larger than the pants covering the

basketball belly my mother bequeathed to me.
Sturdy shoes with high insoles to prop up foot drop.

I'm the 18-year-old in a yellow sundress
wearing Straw Hat cologne, breezing

through Disneyland on my day off to pick up
my paycheck at the food stand where I work.

Maybe I'll see that guy who works in the kitchen
grilling burgers. The one who caught my eye through

his horn-rims, smiled as I left work yesterday.
Or maybe I'll see the tall guy from the Matterhorn ride—

tan legs, knees visible between lederhosen and
long Bavarian socks. Or maybe the sandy-haired

sweeper who hangs out across my work station
when it's quiet between customers, elbow on the

counter, broom and long-handled dustpan ready
in case a supervisor comes by.

The day my fallopian tubes asked me to play hopscotch

The fire carries on with the logs.
Clearly there's something going on between them.

If our lives are stanza breaks,
little rooms inside a house,

can we really discern
which room we'll next enter?

—Go ahead. Pin a dance on me.
I'm turning into an Autumn leaf—

The day my fallopian tubes ask
me to play hopscotch

is the day my rambunctious expletives
will burst into lava.

What Eve Told the Snake

It's comfortable here, you know.
They got me this La-Z-Boy rocker-
recliner, with the swivel base. All
I gotta do is drop one toe
to the ground teeming with bugs
and *push*, to spin around, survey
this Eden. Now Adam, he's wandering
around naming, naming, naming
the multitude of plants and animals
but it's tough, you know, since
we didn't first invent *language*.
Who can remember those sounds
that spark the memory,
to actually *invoke* the toad, raven,
hyena, the poppies, the anteater?
Not to mention those things without
touchable forms, you know, sunlight,
the wind, the fog. And how about
writing? How will we remember
what we named the hedgehog yesterday?
We haven't even figured out
vowels from consonants. We
are so getting ahead of ourselves.
What's next? Crossword puzzles?
God created everything, and now
we gotta do the paperwork.
Won't you slither under the gate here,
Snake, and flick the latch
with your forkèd tongue?
I want to go to town,
check things out.
Get my nails done.

Reflection

Late August
late afternoon
two ravens riding thermals

hills on tawny haunches
scrim of breathless oaks
pond that holds it all and gives it back.

Feels like we're in a painting
says a child
minnows at her feet

and now we are.

How will I die?

after Judy Chicago

Will I die in my lover's arms?
　　Nope. All long gone.

Will I die curled up with my cat?
　　No. She was in too much pain. I had to put her down.

Will I die the way I was born?
　　No. *Twilight Sleep*'s no longer in use.

Will I die in a hospital hooked up to tubes?
　　(See health care proxy.) The DNR is on the fridge.

Will the *Death with Dignity* initiative
　　come to mind
　　when it's my time to go?

Or will I die like my neighbor Frank
in a chair by the window after lunch?

(We'd pulled our clothes from the dryers the day before.
　　He'd showed me how to fold a fitted sheet.)

Or will I die in a car or mowed down by a car?
More likely the latter, I'm an aimless wanderer,
flatfooted, head in the clouds.

In Driver's Ed, the summer I was 16,
Mr. Bender took over the steering wheel, said
Karen, you don't anticipate.

The Coming of...A Certain Age

She becomes more ghostlike each day, even
her footsteps make barely a sound, just this
soft patter, almost nothing—a big cat late

for the kill, arriving after the delicacies (the
heart, breasts, & thighs) are gone, leaving only bones
to content her. She sees herself consisting, not of

flesh & frame, but layer upon layer of memory, the
strata of time upon time, an airy, eccentric body
near to undetectable, a wraith lacking vital shine.

Unlike her blossoming days: she'd enter a room and
the temperature would rise—then, she was tomorrow's
candle impatient for a match, impatient to dust

off the stars within her and emit a light that flares
into the little-known, the un-nameable, into
any tomorrow. Now, taking in a breath,

she lets out something like a sigh, sending
not a prayer or demand (more a reconciliation) up
toward the heavens (whatever that might be) a warm

exhale of hopes & defeats as though they were bouquets
tossed by a bride. She throws another, and another, free of
expectations, the light within her igniting the air.

With end words from *The Coming of Light* by Mark Strand

Edges

Stepping into the quick chill of early evening,
paths dotted with the gleam of solar lamps
and the overcast sky a shadowy white
above dark streets, the high, keen cricket call
says Fall. I know these days, as the sun
slides lower in the sky, and the haunting
scent of wood smoke hangs briefly at the edge.

This is an edge in a life full of edges. Moments,
days when a corner turns, new breath
is taken, a loss mourned, a voice welcomed.
Times when grief and joy mingle as change
shivers before it pounces.

Four early autumn days before my father
died he called, wished me happy birthday.
I released the phone—hot faced, heart full
that he had thought of me. The day my baby
bundled like a bun, gazed at me steady,
suddenly quiet from her red-faced bellow.
The day I climbed into my aging Volvo
to start a thousand mile journey south.

There is an edge between soft sand and
billowing ocean, earth and sky, song and silence.
A point of hover as two meet, a place where
my edge touches yours, where life is full.

Rocketdyne, 1959

Woodland Hills, California. That's
where we shagged, burnt orange carpet,
olive green rug. Our wet bar's gold-veined
mirror reflected a tall piss-colored
bottle of Galliano Liqueur, spirit
of the Harvey Wallbanger,
Golden Cadillac.

Across the cul-de-sac they rented
their mid-century ranch for porn shoots.
Let's film in the laundry room,
you be the Maytag Man. There was fantasy
in The Valley, skies graced by the Rocketdyne
test missiles curling colored smoke trails.

Rocket engine research and atomic reactors
in the mountains above new tract homes
where children played in the dirt.
The Santa Susana Field Laboratory
reactor released a massive cocktail
of plutonium and strontium.

We didn't know the atomic reactor
malfunctioned. Outside our sliding
glass doors, there were celebrations,
the sound of the sonic boom
and the lingering evidence of the rocket
launch—a candy-colored veil of spent fuel.

At the Beach, When Suddenly, I

Was thinking to hang it all up
Thinking I've written myself bored
The well dry but
The day stellar, I mean there was a hot sunshiny
Clarity you could see for miles
Beyond knotted troubles and I carried a good book
When suddenly
Fog
So thick we're talking mythological
Fog dropped down like a stage set
Obscuring swimmers boogie-boarders surfers
Fog
Obscured lifeguard rescue boat eclipsed
Shadows
Brown pelicans flying low
Figure eights ancient as morse code
They intuit something
Serious
Bellwether brown wings warning
Like the bottom of every
Cup, the dregs are screaming
And I don't know how to write disaster.

Changing Names

Since I was born female,

I've grown accustomed to the unstable
nature of my last name. It first changed
when I gave up my virginity and gained
a husband.

It again changed when we took his Italian
name to court, and with the snap of a gavel,
a dark-robed judge returned it to its original
Italian roots.

When my husband left our marriage,
he gallantly left his name behind,
which matched in triplicate
the last name of our daughters.

All three girls grew into women
who fell in love and stood
at the marriage altar for their own
female name-shedding ritual.

They untied their father's name and tied new
knots with their husbands' names, leaving me
moored with a name that's not really mine,
not now my daughters, not ever my heritage.

Do I even remotely *look* Italian?
But it's blatantly still the name my ex-husband
bears, and ironically the same name
his now ex-wife still shares.

In this bounteous wonderous land where I'm free,
what kind of old tangled logic can yet still bar me
from embracing a personalized, individualized,
and splendiferous last name?

So on this picturesque balmy and sunlit beach day,
with surfers and seashells and blue waters waving,
I'll grab that old surname, and with a hearty *Heave Ho*
toss it far over seafoam—and choose a name all my own.

Driving the Pacific Coast Highway

Top down
wind in my hair
waves on the right
hills on the left
Beach Boys blasting.

That's the fantasy.

The reality is
less romantic—
a minivan in
stop and go traffic
trying to make it to LAX
in time for a flight.

We pass a Moreton bay fig
gnarled roots below
a canopy of branches above.
A couple on a blanket
embrace in its shade.
I long to be that couple
on that blanket
under that shade tree.

What?
Nothing.
What did you whisper?
Just...I hope we make it.
To the airport?
Yes. That too.

Baby Blue Eyes

Nemophila menziesii

This morning we passed under a Tree of Heaven
            and onto the rocky upriver trail. All around us were names
                        I had forgotten, so I recited those

I still knew: foxtails, brodiaea, wild oatgrass, brome;
            and the butterflies: pipevine swallowtails, painted
                        ladies, the mourning cloaks, which fluttered

on just ahead of us, our mascots and guides—
            some sunning on warm schist, or hugging the lit blades
                        of spring grasses. The fresh new spears

of weeds thrust up jauntily between the uneven cobbles of river
            stones as we marched lightly on through a fresh scatter
                        of baby blue eyes, the *nemophila* John Fremont

compared to California skies. *Be careful*, you joked,
            your own eyes a clear baby blue. *Can't you hear them crying?*

Fire Drill (Santa Rosa, California, 2017)

At bedtime, no hint. Sky clear.
Moon rising. House built like a boat.
Wine Country hills a lullaby of waves.

Attachments spill from small rooms—
tatami mats, heirloom glass, a seventeen-
year-old cat. Broad decks echo parties past.

The retired couple thinks of other five-alarm nights.
Repeats these mantras: *Eleven miles is so far away.*
Smoke smell, no flames. No official order to get out.

When a daughter phones at 10 p.m., they pack,
then sleep, only to startle awake at midnight
with her second call: "You must leave NOW!"

Registering the red sky, siren winds, flickering
ridge, they start the car, drive fast downhill,
then meet a wall of flames. Turn back.

Back home, they place a panicked call to 9-1-1.
Dispatcher says, "GET ANYWHERE SAFE!" They run
to the pool next door. Balance on the edge. Jump in.

Gasping air through soaked shirts, watching the world
burst into flame, standing back-to-back, they ask,
How long does it take a house to burn down?

All night. The night they could have died.
Wind keening. Propane tanks exploding.
Timbers crackling. Air buzzing embers.

For six hours they hold each other. Shiver.
Cry. Think of family. Say, "I love you. I love
you. I love you." Miraculously, survive.

Pulling themselves out of the pool, they greet
the sepia dawn. Survey their home's charred ruins.
Grab hands. Walk away through smoke and ash. Go on.

Dear Nephew, Where IS Rock Bottom?

Island crushed shells beneath
our feet, as waves sideswipe
the coral reef

We freckle in the sun,
hover over parrot fish
clear our masks with spit

You dive into velvet water,
golden boy in a trough
between swells that shine like opals on fire

Your breath streams
whorls of bubbles, you rise
legs, lungs, zeal and mettle

erupt twinkling with gifts:
nautilus, cowry and whelk
from the floor of heaven.

I can't remember when you stopped
swimming, when the perks of privilege
became smack-filled syringes.

Now you crave limbic hush
like the old rush of ocean, needle-prick, high tide
coming in between your toes.

As coral reefs crumble to white powder, we
are long-distance-lifeguards, watching you
flounder in depths that drown us.

Where on earth is the perfect prison,
where they bless you with Jesus and new teeth,
where you surface and catch a fathomless breath?

Looking

The War has been going on since just before Christmas. It's February now. I'm four years old, sitting between my parents as we make our Sunday trip to San Francisco to visit friends. We drive from San Mateo along El Camino Real. In San Bruno we approach the Tanforan Race Track.

Suddenly Dad orders me: "Don't look!" Mom pushes my head into her lap. As I duck, I steal a peek at Tanforan.

Families stare back at me from behind a chain link fence. They're dressed in Sunday clothes like me but they have suitcases like they're going on vacation. I ask what they're doing. Are they waiting for a Greyhound Bus?

"They're Japanese," he tells me. "Most of them OK but some might do what their emperor tells them. And we're at war with their emperor. They have to go away where they can't do any harm."

He tries not to sound scared like the time I almost fell in our fish pond, but I hear his voice shake. "We shouldn't talk about it." He speeds up.

Mom says, "I'm sorry you have to grow up in War Time."

Years later I learn that most of those families were interned at Topaz, Utah, in the Mars-like desert of the Great Basin. Now my own family stops for lunch in the nearby town of Delta on the way to visit grandparents in Colorado. Oblivious.

In 2019 my son's family including teenage daughter Emily make the same trip and take me along. We slow down in Delta and I notice a large new building along the highway. The sign says Topaz Museum. I insist we stop so Emily can go in. I tell her what I saw as a four-year old.

I want Emily to look and to see.

Are We Aging Out of This Scene?

I remember the old days back in Chicago
our musician friend who played two hundred gigs a year
with her family band got a reminder from her husband:
—*honey, I don't see myself performing at seventy*

my fiddler husband and I laughed at the absurdity—
who could imagine taking the stage at such an ancient age?

but when that distant time arrived for the two of us
the question had to be faced
—*are we aging out of this scene?*

fiddlesticks! what nonsense! our audience can expand
(or contract) as easily as my accordion

who needs a stage or crowded clubs
we still have farmers' markets   retirement communities
even nursing homes

then maybe we move to Toronto closer to our married son
play for a grandkid or two if we get lucky
at night we might shuffle down to the corner pub
sip lime and tonic (hold the gin)
offer up some hot Cajun tunes in exchange for dinner and tips

or perhaps we find one of those havens for lively but serene elders
like that new Zen place here in California

whatever comes our music will sustain us
we will keep playing as long as we can for ourselves
for our aging fellow travelers

and for the younger ones who watch and listen with indulgent smiles
never guessing their moment will come
sooner than they think

Winter Wallop

The mountain fell into the road,
the road fell into the sea, cypress
fell along the fence line,
and I, into reverie. Blue
sailboat dissolving in haze,
scent of black sage on my sleeve,
rocks clacking in the backwash.
I fell into the romance
of everything changing.
The way California is always
shifting, cracking open new veins
of gold, grinding out high peaks.
It did not feel like loss, but
a wheel turning. I felt this
even as my friend
lingered in his blue cotton gown,
amid mists of antiseptic wash
amid the mechanical whoosh.
Even then, I studied the landscape
and spoke of love
though love fell on me, like loss.

1958 Fruit Cutting Shed

In that sweltering tin shed,
at my place at the table,
I learn about cruising, French
kisses, and the Ronettes.

I am nine years old,
a new knife
and sack lunch of salami
clamped in sweaty hands.

My pay: a quarter
per enormous lug box.
I cut peaches
from daybreak to dusk.

Children stand on pallets
slice sticky fruit,
sing with the radio
as sulfur fumes sting.

My future husband,
the ten year old shed boy,
removes layers of peach halves
when I shout "Trays away!"

June, July, August...
I earn less than ten dollars.
My fingers harden,
bleed.

I Saw My Mom Today

I brushed my teeth
and washed my face.
When I rinsed away the soap
(Ow)
from my eyes,
there she appeared
to my surprise

I saw my mom today

As I inspected my lids, my lips, and nose
and wrestled a stray, white bristle
(Ugh)
from my chin
much to my chagrin

I saw my mom today

I filled in my now sparse brows
Where did they go?
Plucked into submission,
I suppose.
(Sigh)
Nevertheless, I drew friendly commas
above my eyes, just like Mama's.

I saw my mom today

As I applied my daily regimen, the
anti-oxidant,
anti-aging,
anti –
(Oh-the-heck-with-it!)
and added a bright red swipe
just below my nose.
Purse. Pucker, now pose.

That's her smile for sure.

I saw my mom today.

Joan of California

Before the wedding, Joan savors the sweet
of sweaters, cashmere & pearls. Dreams of
becoming a teacher in LA. On weekends she
sketches, coloring in the Pacific with turquoise
& azure oils. Water rich with song, she loves
the wide of it, how waves morph into shore.
At 18, Joan likes sock hops, The Texas Twist,
& Elvis. She collects 45's, records. In Hawaii,
she rides tandem in the Makaha International
Surfing Championship. Never surfed before.
Stranger's hand on her foot, wild orchids from
the Waikiki hills, strung together, worn around
her neck in triumph. After the wedding, a heartbeat
forms in water. Belly grows. Not planned but
wanted, she says. My body sprouts roots
in the meat of her soul. Like a trespasser, I
feast on bones, pink as a dawn, rising. I
grow strong & wild in the gold of her.

*

Mother, let me learn to paint
the world the colors
of a California sky.

The Way I See It

When hundreds of small black birds tremble
the water's skin like vermin
you know you've got a jaundiced eye.
Besides which you've got transmission lines
on rust hills. Dusty tamarisk. The wind. And black,
barren the mountains. Dwarfed, mere hills
as though geologic liposuction
reduced them from the center long ago.

By *you*, of course I mean *me*. And believe me, I try.

But I see no miracle in your (and that's *your*, not *my*) baby.
How can I be impressed
with a being that can only grow to be something
that is very much like you or me?
Two eyes, a nose. Those little fingers and toes
that so impress you. I have the same and so do you.

Ah, jaundiced eye! The membrane slides away.
I see:
A lizard doing pushups on the rock. So different
from me it can be no other thing than Life itself.
Fingers, toes, eyes and mouth. A pulse.
A miracle.
Its heart pumping, and mine that had closed down, armored,
        explodes open to beat—beating beating—again.

Lizard, lifted from the rock, throat pulsing.
Cold-blooded in my hand.
Fingers cling.

Kindling

California is kindling to the world.

The coast leans toward the Pacific
and to the left.

We light the fires of thought
which takes the rest of the nation
years to discover.

We are stereotypical suns.
Bacchus blessed us—
The fruit of our vines
reach every continent.

We are black, brown,
yellow, beige, tan,
but mostly green.
We are here to change the world
by being our collective selves—

Melding our various cultures and languages
into one optimistic hope for the future.
We may burn and shake at times,
but we come up shining.
For us, despite the challenges,
we know we live in Paradise.

California, My Ground

I arrived at the Port of San Francisco on October 15, 1962. A year old, I'd sailed with my Japanese mother from Kobe, Japan to reunite with my American father, who'd traveled ahead of us to begin graduate school in Claremont. I have no memory of that long sea voyage, nor of our land journey to the Pomona Valley, but I know that first migration is forever imprinted on me. Since then, I've left and returned to California four times. All told, I've lived and worked in California for roughly 48 of my 63 years, and no matter where I've lived or traveled, California has been my spiritual base, my ground—the place where I feel most like myself.

As a mixed-Asian, bicultural woman and Third Culture Kid who grew up in Southern California, Guam, and Japan and was profoundly shaped by all of these places and their histories, I feel most mirrored in California — perhaps especially in the Los Angeles area, where I've finally settled. From my '60s SoCal childhood, I have memories of coastal road trips, visits to Disneyland and Little Tokyo and Olvera Street, Santa Barbara's Old Spanish Days, and birthday celebrations in public parks. But like a true TCK, I feel love for both SoCal and the San Francisco Bay Area, where I lived for 28 years, and where I met and married my husband. Across many moves, and stints in Tokyo and New York City, my adult self has called Long Beach, Los Angeles, San Francisco, Oakland, El Cerrito, Richmond, and now Pasadena *home*.

On the brink of a new national era, I have faith that our state will continue to support young people and immigrants, work to protect our wild spaces and further the arts, and strengthen our social, cultural, and civic fabric.

A Time for Everything

Three decades ago a friend gave me a coffee cup
for my birthday.
She thought it was special. The color. The design.
I was younger then, maybe too young
for its muted splendor. I wanted louder, brighter,
splashier. Maybe tropical flowers, parrots,
butterflies. A color I could feel in my gut
like lust. This cup didn't speak to me,
at least not above a whisper.
Still, I packed it and brought it with me
when we moved from Israel to Los Angeles.

The poor gift gets pushed to the back of my cabinet,
neglected for years as I drink from more colorful cups—
and later from the treasured mug my grandchildren made me
and the black one with a photo of my son and granddaughters—
until today when, suddenly, it catches my eye,
and as I pull it out and hold it,
I find myself falling in love
because what could be more beautiful
than this faded golden yellow
rounded mug with a cream interior?
I choose it now, ready—in this world of war
and hostility—to drink coffee from a cup that
radiates quiet and calm and subtlety,
plain as the manilla envelope that holds my poems,
not a color that calls attention to itself,
not bright like daffodils or marigolds or buttercups,
but warm and mellow like the wisdom
held close to the heart of an older woman.

Lost and Found

The muddy trail
  leads me through silence
    and thunder and regret
A scattering of seed cones
  and acorns, shade-damp
brimming with fern and frog song
  slash piles from last year's timber harvest
Here is where I listen to wind
  and to the voices of my grandmothers
Here is where sycamore leaves
  turn metallic sun sparks to oxygen
My shoes grow thick with mud,
downhill into memory
  of where the children mixed potions
from blackberries and sage
    (before they grew and flew)
and my beloved bushwacked to winter's waterfall
  (when he was able)
Today, I'm alone on the path,
  following a swallowtail butterfly
    over tangled roots and rodent burrows
  I willingly suspend fears of puma and bear,
    notice a splotch of lichen the color of lime
  the canyon blurs all sense of human-clocked time
Climbing uphill, wind-whooshed and earth-held,
  heart clear
    I claim each step
  in fragile gratitude.

Happy About It

"[A] leader without followers is simply a man taking a walk"
—John Boehner, Republican House Speaker

Just me taking a walk, no followers,
& happy about it.
No dinner slow-cooking,
& happy about it.
No writing in hand,
& happy about it.
No prize in sight,
& happy about it.
No memoir to tell,
& happy about it.
No grandchild option,
& happy about it.
No horizon to fly to,
& happy about it.
No hot tub in California,
& happy about it.
No Amazon Prime,
& happy about it.
No artificial intelligence app,
& happy about it.
No facelift, no Botox,
& happy about it.
No award for retiring,
& happy about it.
Life is taking a walk,
& happy about it.

Small, far-off, shining

night sky

thoughts flicker

satellite

or planet

planet

or plane

point on a skew

line

reels my attention

on filament the color of water

or air

flickers like a name

forgotten in a breath

remembered

some night when

faithful clouds

come between us

and constellations

beclouded even on clear nights

by multicolored flares

lights of a city

run aground

Taking Selfies with My Older Sister During Spring Thaw in Minnesota

Her memory has become a little
like melting snow. Dreamlike, a few years
since we've been together, time is an origami bird
folded in on itself. Flying frightens her,
as does the field behind my house in California
she does remember. Any minute it could catch fire.
Worse, it could bury me
like the one on the news. *You should think
about moving back. You should think...*

She repeats everything at least twice.
Once a nurse, she's used to giving advice.
Next thing, we're both kids and mother appears.
My sister's litany of old miseries darken
her room in the complex where she's come
to live in her 80's. *But she loved us*, I say,
between storms. I show her latest pictures

of my grandchildren on the iPhone, and one
I just clicked walking along the Zumbro river
outside her window. Two ducks feed
over the reflection of leafless trees.
Let's take a selfie to remember today, I smile.
Face to face, cheeks touching,

I snap one picture
after another. She laughs as long ago,
not that, not that. Our chatter disperses
shadows, echoes down the long hallway
of closed doors.

She chooses a favorite. *Not bad
for an old lady*. I suggest two ducks,
going with the flow. She repeats,
going with the flow. I brush a feather-strand
of hair from her damp face in this age
where everything gets saved. Someplace.

Royal Scandia

I lie in the hammock behind our Valley rental refuge. Pool and sky multiply oblongs of opal, watched over by pushupping lizards, four scaly inches of tough. Green blades flit forever since the hardhat men gave the grove her cheap haircut, barren wires loud now with bird blare. Occupants next door slam the dumpster, to let us know that if we aren't respectful, they'll smoke near the cinderblocks, blow cloudbanks of dank across our crumbling concrete. But I don't care. I greet everyone, the glowering cell phone bro, the skulking housecoat lady and the trucker-cap gal with her dog-loving toddler named Cali. We're all lucky to be here, with the noble old oaks and coyote cacophony, the pitted pastel cliffsides swooping with swallows. The sign says *Country Club Apartments*. But behind the palmettos rests an older curving font spelling *Royal Scandia*, the original queen of midcentury harmony, chained jewel pendants ambering the stairwell, competing for dazzle with the trans boys' string of plastic cacti. I watch the *S* peel away, day by day. Everyone needs a personal palace, until the day we don't.

How's Your Memory?

First, appeared the chair.
It stood on the stage waiting
to be settled into, or leaned on,
or for the last woman
on earth to step into view
and carry it off and away, stage

left, one shoe squeaking.

The banana had no role, well,
no *speaking* role.
It had three syllables but only
two talents, be swallowed or go brown.
Has anyone really, ever, slipped
on a peel spread like a starfish,

she wondered, like in old cartoons?

Sunrise comes at the start
and Sunset at the end, separated
by one day. If one's anxious
for sunset, a day's long to wait.
But if all you get is one day, that's short,
said Einstein,

sort of, though not in those words.

If a nurse asks, *How's your memory,
any problems?*—Don't try to be clever.
Don't say, Yes, same ones I've always had.
Like, you know how when you're told,
Don't think of Something, you think it?
Since it was her job to remember these

three, now she was afraid she'd forget.

Once, she caught a Broadway song
and got this pair looped in her head,
Sun-r-i-i-s-e/Sunset, Sun-r-i-i-s-e/Sunset...
Today, she's driven ten miles
of City, but can Not outdistance
that tuneless, nonsense-talking trio,

Sunrise, Banana, Chair

Forgive Me

They were delicious/so sweet/and so cold
—William Carlos Williams

I know why William Carlos Williams ate those plums:
so sweet, so cold.
I nearly shoplifted them.
So hungry, so pregnant
that summer in the Black Hills.

The flurry of letters to the cabin on Bluebell Route
chronicles my misery
sixty-five years ago. He would not buy me plums.

My father wrote that sometimes women needed expensive food
when they were expecting (his first grandchild).
He enclosed a check.

His mother wrote that canned food also carries vitamins
a pregnant woman needs. No need for fresh fruit.

So hungry, so pregnant.

I foresaw a lifetime of canned fruit cocktail.
Even if I got all the cherries it would not make up
for those plums, so tart they make you shiver.

So hungry.

Was it then or later I knew I had married the wrong man?
I wanted that one who lived with me in the Garden of Eden,
the one who gave me the apple.

Rickie Lee Jones; Last Chance Texaco

Waif in a raspberry beret
waltzing up to the microphone
like you've got all the time in the world,
your curled mouth full of mischief and longing.
Bad luck the soil your voice was seeded from,
colliding with a hope so vast
it creates its own universe. And I confess:
I too have gotten into cars
where the driver was drunk and stoned and feral.
I too have flirted with peril.
Dumb luck we survived being reckless girls
in a feckless time, though luck's
a fickle wind to depend on.
What was it protected us,
when so many others vanished in the dust?
You resigned yourself early
to the loneliness that comes
when you can be none other than just yourself.
You let us see your pain and your light,
and like always you're serving up the real thing tonight
blood-bright and road-weary,
each line a profane hymn,
and we're waiting for the end when you lean in
to whisper the mercy shot, the coup de grace,
the answer no one will believe.

Unmasked

Surely these lands were once browned grasses, meandering California oak branches twisting up mottled blue. Surely fire orange poppies, milkweed and Monarchs meandered these hills. *Gabrielino-Tongva* journeyed these coasts, lived on acorns and berries born of flat lands and grounds. Now, electric transformers hover treeless abodes, while scrap junkyards, acid batteries, and rotted engines metal these scrawling hills. Now, soured blood, rotting carcasses, chromium scorch acres of ground. Now, blindered hordes barely question what's taken place. Nor what looms ahead. Surely lavender and salvia will dry on their stalks. Surely summer's oaks will brown again into fall. Slaughterhouse animals, sheep proceed staring down at the rails. Shuffling along concrete sidewalks they head into the pain.

the bounty of age

slowing down with the pull of piled years
patterns emerge that eluded us before

racing towards ocean shore waves in youth
meant missing the wind-blown ranges
of hills and valleys etched onto beach sands

slowing lets us see love's ebbs and flows
like gulls moving as winged clouds
around the beach to part as if cleaved
then reunite soaring ever higher into the sky

in the randomness of kelp piled and in wisps
a tale of capitulation and resistance is told

the bounty of aging is
that even as one's eyes weaken
sight becomes more keen

Remembering the Word

Now that I've accumulated some of those
unthinkable birthdays, I carry the unsayable
with me, the words I can't remember that
do not leave to return, but leave to leave

I can only make shapes of my thoughts into
substitutes, replacements, use phrases that
are almost but not quite what I mean

sometimes the word I seek to speak escapes
the tip of my tongue, having set off to store
itself as a cryptic message, a seed in a cistern
buried underground in the secret keep of the
third abyss of purgatory

I've always pulled forth words for what cannot
be said, always knew there were words for
everything but now discover they might not
be in any language I know anymore

in this time of my life, it seems every word
I pick to hurl on the tips of darts with the
speed of life, is the wrong one

the pebble clear bubbles, the unselfing of self
the demonic, diseased, dangerous, exhaustible
with desire the unsayable—said

I'm interested in the power of the unsaid
the gory details and fiery language of the
unspoken and what happens if the
expected words never strike.

Mary Magdalene and the Decline of the California Incline

Waging an honest living is a bitch
so, when the clock strikes five
Mary Magdalene is ready to ditch her cubicle.
With neither the strength nor the patience
nor the muscle for 405-hustle home
she heeds the Pacific sirens luring her west
down the decline of the California Incline.

And then, can it be? Soiled, shabby
looking a lot like her sweet Jesus
begging for another Last Supper.
Blistered, bare feet in need of perfume, a spit
and a shine, He carries a bottle of green Gatorade
and a weathered cardboard sign. Halo encircling
his sun-bleached plaits, she notices

His Radiance aglow on the street corner
under the red neon stop light.
She rolls down the window to stare
into a ribbon of ocean weaving through
empty tombs oblivious to the outstretched
offering of her hard-earned dollar.
How does He like working the streets?

Mary smiles, ruby-tinted shades sliding down her nose.
She waves. "Dude, it's me. What the hell happened
to all your hopes and dreams and paradise?"
He holds up his sign. Fuck this shit!
"Sister Hope is long gone. Faith is lost and Charity
hitched a ride south last year. It's the end of the dream
old gal, don't quit your day job."

A right turn, and He is but a memory
in her rearview mirror as she heads up the coast
over the hill, through Topanga where she'll disappear
taking shelter in the shadows of the valley
with the comfort of her Jeopardy, a Lean Cuisine
and a bottle of Chardonnay,
she will fear no evil.

Listen Baby Boomers

It's time! Fling back the sheets,
get your parents out of bed,
they've been warehoused too long.
I know, my dad is one of them.
Paint those drab rehab walls,
hang paintings, paisley curtains.

Let there be a garden room, light,
cirrus clouds, butterflies.
Let them have a bubble machine,
a silver ballroom, Dixie and Swing,
Crank up the karaoke, *Sweet Georgia Brown.*
Bring on the trumpets.

And for insomniacs —
give them an all-night theater wing,
popcorn for those who can chew,
bonbons for those who can't.

For My Grandson, Isaiah

Last year you were a goofy kid, obsessed
With anime and soccer, obsidian
Hair rooster-tailed, exuberantly dressed.
Now you're a tall, strong man — kind, witty and

Confident, cowlick tamed into a braid.
In the Bible, Isaiah prophesied
Destruction, called us out for all the hate.
You say you are afraid, you need to leave

Our country — it's not safe. I suddenly
See you with their eyes: dark-skinned alien.
I won't rename true fear anxiety.
To say there's no danger would be lying.

We have failed you, yet I'll say this for us:
In the claiming of feeling you're fearless.

Knowledge and Praxis

A late pandemic abecedarian

A cosmetology department flyer on a
bulletin board near the faculty lounge
catches my eye, punctures my inertia.
Damn this dull gray. Damn Covid.
Except for Tom, nobody's touched my
face, my hair for two years.

Give me your finest chemicals. Don't
hesitate. Keep foiling each strand. Even
if your professor steps in, takes charge
just as you turn to my bangs.
Knowledge and praxis coalesce with time.

Let me sit silent under the black cape.
My quiet's no critique of you, dear
novice. No, I'm soaking it all in—
old teacher in a florescent temple,
paradise, really, after so long a
quarantine. Music of blow dryers, voices
rising, someone's Beyoncé ringtone, clink of
scissors, murmur of combs—harmonics
teaching us in this mirrored room how to
unite, how to encircle, beautify each other
versus splintering into posses aiming
words, weapons, memes.
                        By the sink I
exhale, inhale. Do I smell lavender shampoo?
Yes, yes. It lingers long after I
zip my wallet, drive home almost blonde.

Imagine

Horses gallop in the dry brush
as dust rises around them, hackberry, scratch grass,
the mountains beyond.

Endless sky on six sides of us. Wind.

I lift up, tilt along the foothills. I'm old and I love being old.
I'm stiff and sore just from sitting in a chair.

Imagine.

The straight backs of my friends are learning to bow.
I see stars where the woods were.
Angers and their scars line my gut, and there are days
when they still fester.

I wake up clear, mulling the forms that surge toward me,
that slip like angleworms onto my hook.

I do not know much. I never know for sure.
I look for what's there, out there, away over the water.

I Am Santa Ana Wind

When I blow in from Mojave
Old woman wise, thick hipped, cracked lips
I am desert dry, fried egg on granite hot
Seven years thirsty

I am Old woman sly, thick hipped, burnt lips
I shake cinders from my skirts
Rage fires through tumbleweeds
Seven years tinder dry

My breath sends embers flying
Sets flames to chaparral
Snakes and mice hunker down
Dirt is burning

My skirts send smoke rising
I'm scorched dry, fried egg on granite hot
Everything hunkered down or dying
When Santa Ana blows in from Mojave

All I Want, An Ecstatic Death

You are talking to a corpse she smiles.
Patient as a panther on a branch.
her hospital bed looms silent
in the tiny living room.

Bird-thin, radiant
she wears her 60's tee shirt
from the Woolworth sit-ins
in Greensboro. *Going out fighting*
muses her son.

Always put flowers in the vase
one at a time, she taught me that,
her husband arranges the four stalks
of lavender a friend brought. *Lavender*
helps you sleep says the friend.

We recited two of Shakespeare's love sonnets
this morning, we know them all by heart,
they hold hands.

I don't have the energy to entertain you,
she chides the family
poised like a square dance circle
waiting for her call.

Porcelain tea saucers, royal blue
and carmine, cup the pills in careful
order. She sucks down the final potion
through a rainbow straw. A summer breeze
slips in the balcony door. Her husband
leans over her body, a rainfall.

Roll Up the Rug, We Are Dancing Tonight

Dressed in red, the oracle among us
issues a warning clothed in her praise psalm.

What is one breast?
I never asked my grandmother.

> *"A small price to pay for all the living
> and the loving that came afterward."*

Tonight, let us take our love by the hand & lead them
onto the burnished dance floor.

Let our whole bodies sing an ecstatic prayer
for both the living and the dead.

Let us dare one another to burn bright and fast.
May love's blaze be our path to a new salvation.

Mr. Walker

tells me he will help me, keep me safe,
support me. I want to marry him.
Have a wedding, stand beside my aluminum groom.

He is dressed in plain grey tubing
with two rubber wheels, neon green tennis balls
on his feet. His name is Mr. Walker.

There is no where he will not go with me.
We roll the hallway, deck, bathroom. I wear
purple socks with rubber bear paws for traction.

Mr. Walker is serious. But pleasant.
His burnished metal glows with a matte finish,
like a wedding ring, *to have and to hold*.

He teaches me the art of Kintsugi—
mending shattered bones with gold—I begin
to shimmer like Christmas tree branches.

Me and Mr. Walker will spend the holiday
at home by the fire. I will spiral his legs with red
satin ribbon, each step sweet as peppermint.

I pray with Mr. Walker in the holy night
for those in war's way, in terror and tears.
May they know the steady simplicity

of my companion. May we walk them
far from rubble and blood. Bring them here
to our white sheeted bed.

Encounter

Yesterday I had an inkling to take a walk somewhere quiet under a foggy sky by
the sea, and ended up at the Santa Barbara cemetery. I've been reading
Patti Smith's *A Book of Days* where she shares her visits to gravesites with an
homage to birth or death dates of artists and writers, what may have happened on
that day in history. I wandered. I found a bench engraved with the word *Waiting*
which gave me pause, found another facing the sea that I thought my mother's
ashes would appreciate, which I still have. I lingered by a statue of an angel
with her hands pressed to her breast, and met a young graduate from Westmont,
who asked if I was visiting someone special. I said no, but felt called there just
to hang out. So did she. She asked if I believed in spiritual stuff, did the dead talk.
I said I thought the dead did speak, but not to take that too literally. She asked when
they spoke, could I control it. I replied particularly when I write. We spoke of her
future, how things come to us in life—unexpected. She wondered about my career.
I wondered what she went home with. I looked up history for April 14th.
Read it was the tragic date Titanic hit that iceberg, when Lincoln was shot,
marks the Boston marathon bombing, Jean-Paul Sartre's death along with the day
Jackie Robinson was admitted to Ebbets Field in his first major league game for
the Brooklyn Dodgers. It seems fitting to reflect on these large events among the
silent stones and departed spirits. I hope Artemisia finds her calling. I encouraged her
to write, *see what happens*. As Sartre said *"we are our choices"* and *"because we can
imagine we are free."*

Scars

Naked
I stand
before a mirror
exploring my skin
my outsides
the puckers, craters,
lines, blemishes and
yes, even the wrinkles

> I see it all
> or so I think.

My finger finds the scars,
a faded map
on branded skin

> left breast—cancer
> right knee—roller skating crash
> eyebrow divot-shingles
> left cheek-birthmark

The list goes on

> a pooch near my pelvis
> a line near my shoulder
> a burn on my hand

> I see it all
> or so I think
> but what if

I could reach inside
and touch my heart
to trace the hurts that
leave nothing behind
but moving shadows
and slippery memories?

Not so easy
to find my way
in this uncharted place
with no guides or maps
no handholds or railings,
to help discover
what still may need to be seen

> and remembered.

Botanic Garden Built Over a Landfill

Gluttonous bees stagger drunk on fragrance.
I drag my fingers along stem and leaf.

Mint and hyssop, sage and bergamot,
a riot of scent.

In a pond murky with algae
fish trouble the surface.

Saw-toothed succulents reach for sky.
Here and there a bike tire rises.

Tattered doll shoes poke like mushrooms
under notched palms.

Along my path, a few lifeless trees,
some spent flowers, a lost daughter.

How gaudy and enticing life is,
determined to be fruitful and multiply.

Buds, blooms, blossoms, bees surround me.
Beetles, snakes, spears and thorns.

Overhead, hawks circle.
At my feet, the shadows that precede them.

In the Labyrinth

Think of it as music. The cat
is singing to you, not squalling
for his breakfast. He's a violin.
Leaf-blowers on the street below
are saxophones and flutes, that
hammer in the distance is a drum.
Cars pass like harps
rippling in the wind.
High-pitched electronic chirps
of autos waking up
are xylophones. And the man
who starts each morning
with a strangled yell across the street
is a baritone preparing for his solo.

Leave the TV off at night
when street sounds fade.
Footsteps in the hall are lullabies,
some light and quick,
some heavy and prolonged
with staccato coughs and moans.
A child laughs and runs by,
delicate as a piccolo.
Remember desert nights
listening for owl hoot
and coyote serenade. Here
you live too much indoors
but even in this labyrinth
there's song.

Forbidding Fruit

Resigned to wheelchair life, too weak to stand,
She cursed her body, calling it a hearse.
The family stopped eating from her hand
The day she put her mortgage in reverse.
Likewise, her mood regressed from bad to worse:
Restricted diet, ill-prepared and bland,
The mortifying mop-ups by the nurse—
She killed a kind word with a reprimand.

Still, fleeting joy could take her by surprise,
As when she bit into that Bartlett pear:
Sweet recognition danced across her eyes,
Glad juice spilled down her cheek into her hair.
She held the bitten fruit out like a prize
That none, not one of them, wanted to share.

Water Lessons

Once as a child, naked by my tub,
I watched water gush from our faucet,
its steam fading my image in the mirror,
its thrust bubbling my bath with foam.
I marveled at its abundant glistening stream
that seemed an endless glow of silver light.

I wondered how this liquid,
hot for bath, cold for thirst,
obedient to each subtle twist of wrist,
how such a precious thing as water could be free?
What if we had to pay for it like milk that arrived
in bottles weekly at our door!

Of course, I did not know about my parent's water bill
or that this water came from high in the Sierras,
a valley named Hetch-Hetchy, word for grass that fed the Miwok.
Did not know what it cost the Miwok to flood their valley,
robbed of home, community, their link to spirit world,
so this water could flow through pipes to fill my tub.

I knew my water came in pipes, but did not know all
water does not come in pipes - how many women in the world
must carry water on their heads from wells and rivers
or make their living washing clothes along some muddy bank
where flukes from snails that sailed on slave ships
can turn their urine red, make their kidneys fail.

Later I learned how water is abused and must be treated.
How it is polluted, hoarded, stolen from the dispossessed.
How wars are fought for water and the treasures in its depths.
Water, not an endless flow, but finite like our life.
So much in childhood I did not know, yet even in unknowing
at that moment by my tub, watching water flow, I sensed its sanctity.

Ravenous

Now I know why they
feed you after funerals:
crustless sandwiches:
chicken, tuna, egg
great slabs of cheese
juice on a stick: pineapple,
melon, strawberry
raspberries dripping red.

The plates are too small.
My fingers ache to grab and stuff
asparagus, Brussel sprouts, cauliflower
peppers, whole potatoes
slathered with ranch
brie and jam.
Tables too crowded to find a seat
I scarf down a couple of egg salad squares
desperate to cut the line for more.

This woman I knew
was stabbed to death by her son.
I am shaken by a memory of another friend
whom I hid from a murderous husband.
There is not enough food in the world
to fill this trembling void.

I look around for wine
consider coffee
settle for mint tea
dreading a sleepless night.

California

"Are you being sinister or is this some form of practical joke?"
—Allen Ginsberg, "America"

I came all the way out here, and now you're burning.

Flypaper freeways twist and curl, vibrating with trucks

and cars creeping down the off-ramps like mourners

at a funeral. You uprooted all the native species,

replaced them with these blighted palm trees,

knobby-kneed brown hills heaving with quakes.

You used to be so beautiful. Now everything's

a housing tract, eucalyptus and lemon groves

chopped down long ago to build condos

in pre-approved shades of grey or blue.

No more life in the tidepools. California,

the tents of the homeless line every street,

soon to be purged from the pavement

like roaches. Once you were a bride draped

with garlands of orange blossoms, bouquets

of white egrets. How long will the redwoods

send out new shoots, the ocean and the open sky

air their lacy lingerie? Tell me, where is there to go,

now that we have used up this whole Earth?

A Floor Above the Kitchen

I came to old age
which is a floor above the kitchen

where someone is boiling water
for tea.

I came to another season
of war, bloodshed all over

the news. I came to my heart,
still beating, heavy with years

Deer came to the garden,
heads bent to the flowers.

Bees circled my head. The fox,
red tail flashing like a flag, a warning.

I came to a time without thinking,
the past receding like a landscape

-outside the window of a train.

On the Road Again

Forty years heavier, stripped
tires and screws replaced, the Prius
a yurt, my legs a tree pose, lulled
by the labia hum of rubber to concrete,
from the speakers, David Darling on cello.

West Coast smell out the window sweeter
than post-coital, angel clouds trailing and gulls'
old-lady screeches, the siren-sage Pacific a glory
of sequins—the same dye as the mini-skirt
I arrived in late sixties—something's grabbing me.

Past the Laguna roadside stand with the killer
smoothies and avocado-everything I once never
heard of—3000 miles from a Nor'easter history,
and Cat Stevens in the eight-track. *Did I remember
to ask the mechanic to grease the ball joints?*

Past Santa Claus Lane, I catch a glimpse of her
in the rearview—the girl who couldn't find
the exits, scratchy handmade macrame totem
a metronome in her car window, halter top
barely grazing her nipples. Past the no-longer

$6 motel she slept at on top of the sheets—
her fiction of freedom—rooms that spun ahead
of hangovers, night owls demanding names
for the nameless, the ocean's six-beat wave
pummeling. Labor and birth a confusion.

Past Pismo Beach, would I pick up that twenty-
something hitchhiking? Esalen on the bucket list
since the seventies, I'm thinking she belongs there
as much as I do. I'd kiss her greasy forehead, say,
I hear the salad dressing's less salty than semen.

A Stroll Down Main Street

Arches spiral the entrance of this gold rush town
brick inlays in asphalt spongy in summer's heat
native oaks girdled in wrought iron, so they don't escape
greet those off to the Mother Lode.

Once there'd been a saloon, whiskey fights,
replaced by civility, this coffee house anchoring Main Street
with café tables scattered in courtyards of dappled light,
petunias' lipstick blooms tumbling
from noosed pots, palms fan.

Already too hot iced tea small respite.
The fountain contends for Debussy's Arabesque No. 1
cools the retriever's thirst in this dog friendly place.
I'd hope to recognize someone—ghosts
from the past none are in a haunting mood.

My stroll confirms only the street names go unchanged.
Antique stores' wares clutter sidewalks, entice you in the dusty din
where the five and dime once wafted buttered popcorn,
shelves with anything you need and don't
and pennies bought candy.

Hot Yoga studio converts sweat
balanced in Tree poses a
JC Penny's in another time
where I bought my first Beatles T shirt,
and sturdy oxfords scuffing waxed
hardwood floors, dated even in 1964.

Mom's favorite dress shop, a first boutique,
manikins modeling miniskirts, patten leather heels
pastel boatnecks and Mondrian prints all
added to a running tab she'd never hope to pay off.

Boarded up. "Keep Out," the closing eulogy.

The Sadness of Things

...a phrase from Ruth Stone

I have nothing to say about the overgrown plot
where I buried the cat—a secret

only I remember. Or the emptiness
in the sunroom corner where my odious

one-winged parrot lived for fifty years.
This living room: I raised my children here,

their broken ghosts accuse me
from the corner of the gritty settee.

Listen, there's a dull hum
in the unplayed piano, some

might call it Song. Nothing I say
is as beautiful or lost. That's the way

of lyrics— as close as we get to the endless
purity of Things, their birth cries, their sadness.

Artemis at 70

For Jay
Santa Barbara, 2025

Strangers, in passing, remark on our beautiful hair.

Yours white, pouring over your shoulders
like the hair of an old sea god.

Mine, a gleaming horsetail down my back.
Why hide the few graces of age?

At midmorning, we pass through the farmers' market,
argue good-naturedly over tomatoes,

bend our heads to sniff garden herbs,
the picture of a long, happy union.

People want to touch us for luck.
They need not know of our treaties, my love,

our quarrels over matters more damning
than the ripeness of tomatoes.

Or the long, storied lives we led
before handfasting. Or how, betimes,

I visit a lonely crossroads under an open sky
where the blackbird sings at dawn

and there, without your knowledge,
sell my long, beautiful hair for a solitary afterlife.

Heartmeat

I sat all day with others' grief—that being my daily occupation.
Each person a new treatise on the ways the heart can break.
Their loved ones dead and absent, their DNA ripped away,
edges all frayed and tattered in those left behind.

I spent all day trying to pick up a thread or two,
left work tired-sad and came home.
Lying flat on my bedroom floor
my hands crossed over my sternum,
trying to quiet the pounding mass within.

Seeing inside a great slab of meat
raw, red, scored with a butcher's knife,
not beating but still alive—raw meat, bleeding.
A strange image for a vegetarian
but entirely mine.

Crying Room

Mothers with babies and young children are expected to sit inside a small, sound-proofed room—so as not to disturb other patrons. I often watch Westerns through its glass wall smudged with finger prints, enveloped in the lingering smell of wet diapers. I sit between my mother and two younger brothers who don't cry so much as argue, pointing their stubby fingers, Kapow! Bang! Bang! at the bad guys. Fathers never enter the crying room; they arrive with wives and children, then sit undisturbed in the good seats. When I turn seven, I'm allowed to take myself to the Saturday matinee. There, in 1958, I finally sit alone in a good seat. I don't remember the movie, only the poster for the coming attraction: *Attack of the 50 FT Woman*. In garish colors it portrayed a raging giantess. A towering, red-haired, buxom warrior clad in scant satin underwear, she straddled the Hollywood freeway, cars upended beneath her thighs. The giantess looked so eerily like my mother—her hair, her body—the way her face morphed into an evil mask when she had too much to drink. And why did she? Years after her death—even today— her shape-shifting haunts me. Generations banished to the crying room, how early our anger must have risen like a giantess from our small bodies.

Hummingbird

Flat as a stamp you lay on the pavement.
Sparkling like crushed diamonds, sapphires,
rubies and emeralds. Your stilled feathers
glistening in the sun as if you were still
breathing.

The filminess of wings, invisible in flight,
spread as if waiting for death to leave
in order to lift you once more to
the nourishing nectar of flowers.

Gently, I lift you knowing I cannot
throw you in the trash bin.
Befitting your elegance, I take you
home, put you in a tiny yellow
gift box, wrapped in blue ribbon,
adorned with an orange paper flower.

I will find a proper resting place as lovely
as you were. Filling a white, porcelain vessel
with potting soil, I gently place you on
the top, sprinkle more soil over you.

I scatter Lily of the Valley seeds so
they can absorb your essence as they grow,
returning you to beauty through the sweet
scent of their white, bell-shaped blooms.

Shall I place the flowers on the porch so the
cat that swatted you from the feeder,
knocking you to the driveway, as a car
drove by, can eat their poisonous petals?

My Guardian Angel, Sadie

after Ron Salisbury

I pour birdseed from a plastic bag
into empty Clausen pickle jars.
Some of the seeds spill.
Sadie's sigh is angelically soft.
She wears a babushka under her halo,
a shawl covers part of her wings.

Sadie watches me struggle shutting
off my electric tooth brush,
squirting too much sun block out
of the tube, too little spray
on my frizzy hair.
She sees me counting Xanax,
snipping whiskers off my chin.

She's been with me since I was
eleven with two broken front teeth
from a bicycle accident when I rode
into a car. I wore silver crowns
that looked like fangs. Sadie walked
me home from the sixth grade dance.

Birth control pills, lovers I don't
remember, divorces, a miscarriage
and now this, old age, no hand strength,
losing my keys, my glasses, my pens.

Sadie says I'm lucky to be here so long.

Kind of a Book Club

We rarely discuss the book assigned.
The book jacket or book review will suffice.
I hold my tongue even though I'd prefer something
more literary. I ride the ebb and flow
of conversation, the hum of camaraderie.

My younger friends don't ask my age because
frankly, they don't give a damn. Together
we commit to being vulgar and conspiratorial.
We talk about the men we love,
convulse when someone mentions flatulence
at the most romantic moments.

We agree it's okay to be vain, fear thinning hair,
weight gain, and sexual indifference.
Someone mentions chocolate as an aphrodisiac,
better than sex some of the time, under some
conditions. *Comme ci, comme ça,* we toast.

Seems I get wind of political scandals before anyone else.
We dig in like vultures, chew on the subject
until we start to gag. I realize there must be better topics
and being the eldest, suggest a few. We discuss
a calendar of our birthdays, which software helps
avoid overdrafts, how we hated to work
for someone else. Everyone rolls their eyes.

I laugh til I cry.
Humor is the most addictive of all.
Time stands still when I'm laughing.
That's when I feel as young as they are.

The Skater Lusts

If I were a skateboarder I would come,
jiz on my pants as I stare at that hill.
Hands and feet vibrating. My throat is numb.
The grade, the angle — a battle of will.
The fourth steepest street in San Francisco
taunting me with its magnificent lift,
seductive as the goddess Kalypso —
her body offered — a dangerous gift.
I could bomb this menace for seven years,
crouching low, a wolf mounting his prey.
Pushing aside my doubt and my fears,
terror and triumph are slamming today.
I lied. I wheeze as I hoof down Ripley Street.
The truth is daunting, yet the lust — so sweet.

Permanent Summer

Sunrays break the blue dome kettling
Tahoe basin in heat. High temperatures
scorch thirsty sugar pines, the boned
branches of cedars and firs. Straw-like
needles snap and blanket the brown forest
floor, soil crumbles until dust frames
the shore in powder, the ground gasping
for rain or snow. Bears fat with calories
consumed from July and August linger
longer in the high country with no detection
of seasonal change. Just more time to relish
these afternoon rays. Even the aspen jingle
their green-gold discs against the cobalt
lake's sway, undecided about climate's
timing. All around me the land argues for
summer in October. I dress sleeveless,
sporting shorts to recline on an empty
beach. Sweat forms on my neck as I lie
beneath an intense sun, swishing my feet
in tepid waves. For a moment I forget
where I am, lulled by swelter to believe
I must be lazing on a tropical seashore.
Except I am here, sunbathing in autumn
Sierras. I feel as if I am cheating earth's
turn towards winter. Could it be that
this glorious day of alpine heat signals
more than just a hot spell, the long
forecasted warming of earth? How it
sneaks up like a bad spirit to tantalize,
then leaves a wake of chaos. I bolt
upright, picturing earth altered, all of us
bewildered by a permanent summer.

Love Letter

My therapist
wants me to write a love letter
to the girl I was
when I was a kid

I take out a pen
and promise myself
I can do it this time

but all I see
is a girl in a glass coffin
who knows exactly how
to fold her hands

she knows that becoming dead
is the only way to stay alive

she knows that topsoil
can't hide a body's history
for too long

dusk comes

she finally emerges
walks up to me
takes my hand and pulls me
through a dark hallway
towards my old bedroom

I can't promise her
I can stay long
but I can look for a brief moment

I scrawl on the wall
"you will survive this"
but I am not sure
she believes me

I have one foot out the door
but she grabs my hand
and draws a map
of the galaxy on the wall
and whispers to me
"I'll meet you there"

At the Edge of the Pacific

for my brother

Ancient, this sound, the ocean reshaping itself
before my eyes, marbled surf
circling talus and toes. A dash
drawn between your birth and death date.
Ebb: to fall away, to dwindle.
Fathom: to grasp.
Galaxies of days, the hours
hurtling ahead.
Infinite and gleaming is the ocean's trick.
Just look how it curves out of sight,
keels from view and goes on.
Let it. I'll take these
months wound around my wrist,
necklace of bare air,
October's fish-scale sky. The tide's
pull is illusion. I can't
quell the waves or keep them.
Rare: one who is singular.
Slow: how I'll backtrack
toward the living, your ash
unfurled on my fingers, a small
vibration. Salt and its crust
wicked from my skin, no scribbled
"x" to mark what's next.
Yield, you'd say. Submit, as if to the sun's
zenith, its palpable light.

Every Day Is Trick or Treat

Two small children dressed as old people
ring our doorbell crying Trick or Treat

I wonder about the parental guidance here as I
open the door and smile at their adorable little walkers

their funny little old people hats, wigs and spectacles
and I throw some soft chewable candy into their bags

as old people would never be able
to chew the more challenging candy I have on hand

and I wish them a lovely Halloween
and a terrific Thanksgiving

and tell them to be careful crossing the street
as those walkers can really slow you down

and people have little patience for walkers or old folks
I remind them that they have a doctor's appointment

early the next day
not to stay out too late

and once home not to keep
waiting for the teapot to boil

as it surely will given enough time

Boomer Fizzle

I swear to god, in—just pick a year, say 1972—
we were so cool. Hair down to here, all tie-dyed
with rooms bathed in incense, posters
and pot paraphernalia—who'd thought we'd AGE?

We were rockin' the world baby
linkin' arms, while chanting C.I.A.! C.I.A.!
as some ill-suited whitey from The System
filmed our faces on the first
Earth Day.
We marched down main street for Indian Rights
and Women's Rights and Black Power
loaded with liberating language:
War? Hell NO—we won't go!
Just watch—we'll walk on the Moon!
We'd deliver poetry, pizza, world peace
and free love all in one afternoon!

Certain we were on an upward,
evolutionary arc,
the world
forever,
better
Never dreaming
today's news
and weather

Widows & Widowers

Those early days and months
      in the caves of sorrow,
a cold bed that burns the skin,
      long silences broken
by conversations with the dead.

A time when scamsters call
      to cheat a grief-addled brain,
and when appliances break down
      and cars refuse to start—
a curious mirroring of the heart's
      unraveling.

Many stories are heard—
      a man who sleeps in a La-Z-Boy,
unable to bear his wife's scent
      lingering in the sheets,
a woman who sleeps on the edge
      of a mattress, still offering
a dead husband more than his fair share.

Stories about the ones who can't eat
      and those who eat too much,
those who hole up alone for months
      and those at the Justice of the Peace,
their last spouse barely in the ground.

Stories both unique and the same—
      a club for the broken-hearted
            no one wants to join.

Citrus

By which I mean the blossom, not the fruit.
By which I mean the scent and not the sight.
By which I mean nostalgia, its sudden bite.
As if a tree, a patio, a street.
The way the concrete had a fragrance.
The concrete and the asphalt and the quiet, tiny yards.
Because the windows and the curtains.
Because the timbre of a passing car.
And how the dampness of the grass
            in which I meant to pause.
Or when the stippled light on stucco walls.
Because a slow forgetting.
By which I mean the acrid with the sweet.

The Song You Hear at Night

The song you hear at night
is the Pacific.
It's the first thing you see in the morning.
You are no longer frightened
by an unexplainable grief.

What passes for a voice
in the magnified moment
is the song of a cricket.

The lyrics you carved in the sycamore
have already been told,
your late arrival expected
by hooting owls.

The song of sleep:
What have you kept?
What will you keep?
How have you lived?

3:38 A.M.

In grimy Manhattan, once,
when snow absolved the scuzz

and all was hushed, virgin
as a new territory, I was

its first inhabitant. Yes.

Now, climbing out the oven

of the unrepentant San Fernando
Valley, I crest the hill that's sealed off

a cocooning fog—bracing
to feel its chill. Oncoming

lights appear milk-glassed.
The familiar gone foreign.

It's refreshing. To become
a stranger does wonders for me.

At this liminal hour,
I am the only traffic

as I near a chronically clogged
now ghost-town-deserted

intersection, and here,
sitting cross-legged

on pavement—a grown woman
in the turning lane,

staring down the thick sea fret.
Beached, but miles from shore.

Not some tentative stance, no.

She's decided to just be
in the way   for a change.

Words

The heart calls out hidden places of vague impressions, melding them into new perspectives, erasing past convictions by the simple choice of words. Words of every size and contour. Abrupt and staccato, harsh and rough or flowering lightness, fierce, gentle, hostile, loving, nuanced, blunt or a jumble searching for a place to land. Like the sharp bark of a dog or gentle purring of a cat foretell of what is to come, thoughts race through a napping mind, the right words demanding attention and acknowledgement of what is to come. This is why I write. Words falling on an old canvas bringing new color and texture to the tired and practiced. Perspectives shift catching me unprotected and drum me out of safe hiding amid the push and pull of anxiety and relief. It is only thought until written, seen plainly, exposing who I am.

We'd just turned back from the crashing waves,

from the pelicans, their wings opening
and closing like eons, a crow
on a fence post peering past us

when out of nowhere the falcon
appeared. From the placard
I knew she was *peregrine*, traveler.

Without a sound, the crow rose
and like a bouncer the falcon
escorted that bird out of the sky room.

No diving, no swooping, no calling out.

Three weeks ago a blood clot
escorted my friend's husband
to that other sky. It wasn't soundless

and it took longer than the falcon's
task but something made me think
of his death when I saw the space

between the two birds held
constant, then split open, the crow
continuing along the cliff,

the falcon returning
to survey the dune grass,
the wild mustard.

      —for M. M.

Pomegranate Jelly

By November, the slender branches
sagged with dark globes. I cut the stems,
gathered the fruit, and split the husks.
My daughter extracted bright arils
that my son milled on counter tiles
speckled red from the cycling pestle.

We strained the juice through cloth,
added sugar and pectin, cooked and stirred
and poured the boiled fruits of our labor
into hot jars topped with lids and rings.
Fragrant steam glazed the windows
as we lowered the jars by wire rack
into the scalding bath. Withdrawn,
the jars cooled, and one by one, the lids
popped.

Near midnight, my son and daughter
carried their shares to their cars.
They hugged me goodbye
and drove away.
I stood awhile and smiled at the stars
before turning back to the garnet-lit kitchen
brimming with winter gifts.

Love Song for San Francisco, Searching for Disco and Dreams, 1970s

Behind us piles of stone rise, a mountain, sun
in our eyes, scalded before we arrived to the city

whose cement we bow to kiss. Our feet,
are weary of this flight out of passing storms

from Wyoming to Nevada. We are frost bit
with anticipation. The air somersaults

our bodies into pillars. Salt Lake City prayers
fall over us like hail. This is September, we are lost

in the dimming autumn light. The flip
of our words fall over vast roads emptied

of sound. At the Nevada border, long lines
of cars pile up for gas, and we hope the electric

grid will spark, soon. We flee and look away
anxious that this drive-away gas guzzler

will not make it to the next town. Our fingers
bear electricity. We will not fail

even over the passes in the Sierras. We cling
to a California song, the one my dad liked

to sing, about leaving his heart. Nothing
will pick up the pieces of our song, not disco

melodies or a thumping bass, steps I dip into
long before my body had failed. I feel

that we are moving out of a dying,
the jigsaw cliffs of the Rockies

press onto my skin. My girlfriend and I drive
together, as though zooming

into new time zones will help us imagine
there is no hatred trailing behind

our car, like a spy or a gunman aching
to end how we touch.

I Hear This Happens Everywhere

Wonky white blood cells.
A second test.
Waiting.
Even more wonky. Nine
vials of blood lined up
like a row of solders,
my name stitched on every shirt.
Along with my birthdate
eighty-one years ago.
Not TB. Not Hep C.
Three contestants left standing:
Cancer/autoimmune/chronic infection.
Pick one, anyone.
Rock, Paper, Scissors
All lead to the same place.
A diminished life. Waiting.
For doctors to call. Hoping
no disaster on their lips.
Waiting. To learn
what's next. Maybe
a bone marrow biopsy
said the somber nurse
with wine on her breath.
Waiting. Can't stay away
from the internet's dark syllables.
Five years. Progressive. No Cure.
Don't trust my body.
Don't leave the house.
Living on the couch
in anxious limbo.
The future on hold.
Waiting. Hoping my life
will start again.

Breasts

We'd trade tales of a farmer's daughter suckling itinerant strangers—about as close to a dirty joke as we could get without screaming, best friends poring over the Sears catalogue, whispering *cleavage* and *decolletage* in accents borrowed from Pepe Le Pew. In cartoons, girls had breasts like torpedoes but I never wanted mine to be weapons, just perky and pert beneath a clinging cotton sweater like Susan Dey's, ripening somehow at night to heavy globes, smooth as honeydews, peeking from beneath a negligee of satin and lace. In junior high we'd rest them on the shelves of our folded arms and dare the math teacher's eyes to drop below our pretty chins. Oh, breasts, you were tempting as vanilla cupcakes, sweet like cherry popsicles, like twin scoops of apricot sorbet! We rode high in our twenties, the three of us, my girls and I, but when the baby came they were mostly for show, plumped up like leavened dough set to rise beneath a clean cheesecloth, yet unable to yield more than a mouthful of milk. In fact they reminded me more than anything, then, of two bald-headed men, swollen with self-importance and demanding your full attention but giving very little in return. Boobies, that's it. But the glory of breasts in their glory! As I step from the shower now, skin damp and ruched like silk, they're like that old whore with a heart of gold from a fifties Western, the rough-voiced gal who ran the saloon and knew when to leave a man alone to drink, Miss Kitty and her twin in from the city, Miss Titty, I guess. Now and then I'll still hoist them up in some spangled contraption and they're like retired show ponies that hear the bugles from a distant parade, that proud, still fine and high-stepping enough to get me past the velvet rope, but come night they'll be like worn-out toddlers, flopping together irritably as I turn on the couch, regretting the heels, that last glass of wine, the stolen cigarette.

Nostalgia

I remember the sound
of streetcars rumbling on wet tracks
the sight of one pushing
out of the fog
the clatter of coins
as they dropped
through the coin machine
or the hole puncher
biting into a transfer
to be used to board
the next streetcar

I remember the lullaby
of foghorns
the buzzing of overhead
wires for electric busses
the immense sighs
of their brakes
the whoosh of their doors
closing

Ah...what would I give
to be carried away in
a giant rolling cocoon
gazing out windows
neon lights barely visible
through the salty mist
so otherworldly
so like a dream
So what it's like
to go home

Highway 101

I am an artery
I carry the blood of
the living and the dead
past the wild grass and
sand-blown dunes
of this coast, this edge.

North and south I travel.
Built bit by bit,
I go by many names
on my long journey

I have known cities
who grew from seeds
into choking vines and
gathered me into themselves.

I fight to survive on mountains
while they crumble from
under me as they stand
knee deep in crashing surf.

I pass quietly through
green light in
old silent forests,
roll joyfully over hills
yellow as noon
dotted with oaks and cattle.

Yet always I turn
again to the sea.
I am The One.

Death is the mother of beauty

—Wallace Stevens, "Sunday Morning"

A different kind of beauty:
the silence when
rasped breathing stops,
pain-furrowed brow
releases

Your death pushed
me to pen
to write and write and write,
exposing scars—
like manzanita's brown bark
sloughing red

Words
tumble onto pages,
travel through time,
marking years,
marking memories,
fall into poems
bursting like fireworks

Getting Drunk With My Third Mother-in-Law

She laughs like a madam might
having finally found herself
a thousand-dollar john.
She's the only woman I know
who can outdrink me and she
likes me to make hers half vodka
half juice, then two-thirds vodka
a third juice, then she winks, we
drink, communal beasts at the same
watering hole, nothing else mattering.

My first mother-in-law nagged me
for not diapering the baby often enough
my second one didn't like me knowing
that I wasn't a virgin but my third one
just wants to laugh and have a good time.

Once the two of us, alone on barstools
drinking gin, she told me her first husband
walked out on her, the second one beat her
and I told her my second one beat me, too
tried to kill me with his bare hands
and my third mother-in-law
looked me straight in the eye
for the first and last time
and told the bartender to bring two more

and not so much juice this time.

Secrets

My mother was a keeper of secrets
They dwelled in her dormant like soft-spun worms
not quite ready to burst into moth
We didn't know then, my brother & I
that secrets were being kept from us, we only knew
when we approached certain subjects
something in our mother changed
A soft fuzz draped her iris
A slight constriction held her throat
And we, loose-ended, incomplete
asked questions whose answers were pieces
that should fit the puzzle
but didn't
What decided our mother to tell them, these secrets?
doling them out through the years
like stingy drops
from a leaky tap?
Was it our age, or the year,
or a sneaking suspicion that our doubts
had outstripped our belief?
Whatever, they came with a flick of the wrist
like some object carelessly left behind
a stray comb, or a glove
"Oh, didn't I tell you?
My father was Jewish."
"Oh yes, thought you knew. I was
married before."
"That's right. Your brother and sister?
Daddy's not their real Dad."
Each secret burst our lives like
a stone hitting glass
Each secret opened doors,
and shut so many others
Like a double exposure, one photo
bleeding into another
The truth superimposed itself
on the life we thought we had lived
Our childhood only partly our own
and partly our mother's
invention

The Wildland Urban Interface

Fire season starts earlier, lasts later.
Capybaras move north. Underbrush is tinder.
Santa Ana wind whips the blaze.
As the sparks fly upward, we are born
to wildfire and earthquake.

Hemlock and fennel grow taller than men.
Eucalyptus chokes the oaks out. Pinecones
litter ground like grenades. Quail strut, deer freeze,
pileated woodpeckers knock hollowly.
One night we'll be too old to move fast enough.
Rescuers will find nothing but ash and bone.

Ghost Pine

During the "Stay at Home Order," I had time on my hands and kept wondering if the 25 or so photos I had in the bottom of the file cabinet could find a safe home. These are black and white, from the 1940's and earlier, of residents at a nearby Indian Rancheria in Auburn, California. I received them from a retired librarian when I was doing ethnographic field work. I had a very knowledgeable Maidu woman helping me with historical details. This was 1972 to 1974. Concerned that the photos would sit another number of years, I didn't quite know what to do with them. *They don't belong to me, not mine to keep.* Looking again, they include women skinning deer, men's baseball team, picnic at the Rancheria, dedication of the church, another of children playing with trikes and a toy tractor, and the portrait of a man in a World War I uniform. I realized these are originals, the only copies.

I hadn't been to the area since 1975, and figured the land had been sold; maybe the tribal leaders had an office at the new casino? Checking on google, I found an address and email. Immediately I received a response from a woman in charge of Rancheria history stating that she would gladly receive the photos. I didn't want to mail them and due to Covid 19, decided to drive up and deliver them. What impressed me was the new office complex on a high ridge, a spectacular view of the lake and valley, the many buildings made of sandstone decorated with coral and turquoise design. A few golden oaks and airy ghost pines still grow across the road.

Her response was heartwarming. The photos have been scanned and shared with others to try and identify the residents. I'm so gratified that this piece of history found a safe home with First Nation Maidu whose ancestors existed for hundreds of years—hunted and gathered in small bands, and after "contact," lived in poor conditions, then survived the gold rush and continue to preserve tradition. *The photos don't belong to me.*

Moving Day

Mid Sixties Summer Suburbs

Our family had rented that house forever until dad had one too many arguments with the landlord. Everyone cleaning, throwing out stuff, my dad was full of mad energy, packing up a neighbors borrowed pick-up. It was a thing with me in those days to go bare-foot, guess he hadn't noticed that until today. It got me his stare-down. He asked my mom where are my shoes, why aren't I wearing shoes as he built up a lot of steam. Mom just shrugged, busied herself somewhere else.

All work stopped, get in the car he said and off we went. Parking at a strip mall, slamming his car door, he asked me what size shoes I wore. Was he actually going to buy shoes for me, where would he get them. The only place that wasn't a car parts or hardware store was across the street. The neon sign flashing *HOSPITAL SUPPLIES* another sign that read *OPEN TO THE PUBLIC—NURSES UNIFORMS ½ OFF.*

He came back to the car, threw a shoe box in my lap *put these on*. White nurses shoes in my size. Dad really thought I'd wear white nurses shoes. When we got home I put on my flip-flops and hid the shoe box from everybody, even mom.

Years later I asked why he had done this, he didn't remember any of it. He thought maybe he'd taken me back-to-school shopping once. Like that would ever happen. Bless his heart.

Losing Paradise

Is eight grandchildren from two kids enough? Of the third I rhetorically asked, "Why would anyone want to have children today?" I write about wildfire and water in California, and I'm scared. I was shocked at my question and that was five years ago.

My daughter has five children, all young, close in age, living in Mill Valley on a one-way-out canyon road. I suggested that she park her giant SUV facing downhill. She laughed. I kept imagining "Sofie's Choice." That was before Paradise. I wrote about Paradise. Which would she save?

My dad's family came to California in the early 1850s, the second Jewish family to settle in Santa Cruz. Santa Cruz protected its Jews. The Bay Area didn't protect everyone, but the Jews thrived. Then my dad married a non-Jew. They were on their honeymoon when Hitler invaded Poland. I should have been much older, but they had to make sure the right side won the war before having a half-Jewish baby. Now the rise of intolerance worries me. Are my ¼ Jewish kids and their kids at risk? Under the 1% rule, yes.

I've written about how people came here looking for gold. Why do they still come searching for some mythology of opportunity? It's true for so many who've walked over the border, who harvest our food, who've sent their children to our universities. Bravo. But are they safe now? No.

I write about water in the San Joaquin Valley, how immense agricultural corporations sink wells deeper than all others and suck water for profit. Safe drinking water? At what point did we start worrying about that?

My third child still hasn't had a baby. I can't ask why. I'm afraid of the answer.

Searching for Solid Ground

After five years of drought, I crave to see the rush of water on the Truckee River nourishing the central valley. Navigating my frightening descent down the steep 30 foot trail through a forest of towering Douglas Firs, I step on a stick which quickly rolls out from under me.

My arms flail as I reach out for anything solid to grab until my head hits the ground. I roll head over heels. Embedded rocks punch my back. I smell the fir trees and dirt. With a thump on my head, I come to a dead stop against a log at the river's edge.

As people rush to me, I say, "I'm fine, just shaken up." My friend whispers discreetly, "Are you sure you're all right?" She's also 70 and knows I don't want a fuss. It's so embarrassing.

Come morning, I examine at my aging body, naked before the bathroom mirror. Scratches run down my left side, a large bruise gaining color on my hip, my shoulder blades hurt. A pin prick of dried blood marks the end of the lifeline on my palm and pop Tylenol.

I mourn my once sure steps, my confident stride down the hall, high heels clicking, always recognized by the security guard. Hiking the Sierra without ever a fall. Skydiving over California's iconic landscape once I landed in the arms of the trees, calmly crossing my arms and legs to avoid breaking my limbs.

When you lose control, just breathe and do your best. Like when a neurosurgeon says you have a brain tumor. Like when you learn your mother has terminal cancer. Like when you hold your father's hand the moment he dies. Like when you are falling and the ground is coming at you fast.

I live in California

I prefer to say I live in Mexico, that I live on
stolen land although some say that is just

a *spoil of war*. I like to say names of places
like Bolsa due to the ways it couples: *Bolsa*

Chica, Bolsa Knolls, pretty sounding places,
muy bonita, whatever language you speak.

I like saying *Cucamonga* probably because
saying so is a child's game—cuckoo, cuckoo,

cuckoo—and should California's teachers be
forgiven if they don't teach the history of

the Gabrielino or the names those indigenes
gave to their places? I can think of no reason

to say *Downey*, named after the State's 7ᵗʰ
governor, born in Ireland, seduced by riches

(thanks be to the California Gold Rush), a
backer of slavery in the Kansas Territory, fan

of San Francisco's capitalists. I'd rather say
Fresno—meaning "ash tree" in Spanish; I'd

rather say *Hoosimbin Mountain*, thinking
of the Wintis' buzzard water. I'd rather ponder

the myth about the place in Humboldt called
Loleta of which some local Wiyots, those yet

to be killed off, grin, say "let's have sex" but
somehow words can corrupt in translation.

Memento Vivere

Beneath my feet nothing sleeps: tree bones brittled, upended shrubs spun to tumbleweed, old lakes and ancient beaches wrinkled with valleys where only salt remains. The many mountains flanked with faults push upward only to bear the brunt of wind. Smoke trees with their twigged crowns of gray— all that is baked here— and whatever grows for months without a drop of rain. How is it from all this near death and dying there's a glimmer of green leafing out after the smallest rain, the cactus shaded by its needles. This stillness so old, so used to itself. How it carries on while I sense the fragments of my own wintering landscape, my arms spread out like cold bone branches— precious dust at my back—before me caves, silver needled trees standing guard where once there'd been a door.

An American Indian Elderhood in California

My dad died last year. Walked on, is our word for death in my Native culture. Auntie, dad's younger sister is our elder now, eighty-six. I'm seventy-two, second elder. We are American Indians, mixed-blood Cherokee, Lenape, Seneca. I'm California born and raised.

I don't have pictures of dad's side of the family. The film was overexposed the day we lined up according to our generation. In the first photograph the great aunties and uncles are grouped together. These are my grandpa's siblings, born in Indian Territory Oklahoma, and the line doesn't hold a white face.

The next group is my dad, auntie, and all of their cousins—the first half-blood generation in our family.

My brother, sister, and I stand with the largest group of cousins. We are not full bloods or even half, and yet we're not white and never will be. We stand blinking in the sunlight, in our youth, and I remember thinking someday we would become the elders.

Today I'm doing my best to make better for the next seven generations. Writing, volunteering at the community center, reading books to children by Native American authors, working to make sure Native lives and histories are portrayed with honesty and integrity. Providing stepping-stones for the kids so they can see Native people have respect for our traditional ways, and that we are also real people, working as doctors, teachers, writers, authors. Showing the children that Native American mothers and fathers are regular moms and dads who cook dinner, help their kids with homework, play baseball, and that we are not relics from the past. Making a statement that American Indian people are still here, with our celebration of life past, present and future

Low Pressure Building Off The Coast

The large-bellied old men in swim trunks
stand up to their ankles in the ocean, the ocean flat
and hardly moving. They are waiting
for the young men to come home from war.
They rub a little water on their elbows.
I am the youngest in the circle of kids
around Dickie's father.
He lies propped up in the sand without his leg.
One at a time he lets us touch his stump.
I can still feel the slick cool of pulled skin
and the roughly stitched pucker at the end.
That's me in the snapshot, sitting in the sand,
opening my mouth on my knee and tonguing it,
tasting the salt.
Even in black and white, you can tell
there was no sun that afternoon,
the wind light and worrying.

A Sierra Memoir

I enter Lake Basin Trail, breathless at 8000 feet,
eager for the company of lodgepoles,
Jeffreys and firs,

melodies of Hermit Thrush as they call to each other in late
afternoon, the roar of waterfalls cascading to twin lakes
my face damp from spray.

I imagine myself an eagle, fly down the rocks
with a view of another forest and range.
Several people gather

when the angled sun graces each particle of water. Pine
needles crunch under feet as I join others, settle on granite,
patient to savor the evening.

Mercury shifts the following day to cold wind, angry, fierce.
Tall spruce sway like cathedral pillars in an earthquake.
I tremble at the rush through dense branches,

hammering windows. Intermittent calm deludes us
this rage exhausts itself, but clouds stretch sideways,
tipped in white,

rise dark and heavy. Water drives everywhere.
The mountain image dissolves into one
of tainted gesso.

In a few hours, clouds disperse. Light
glitters every cone and stream.
I return to the trail.

Your Mouth and Mine

I miss your mouth. My mouth does. I miss longing for what our mouths could only do together. Weeks after meeting, unable to wait a moment more, I led you to the redwood grove up the hill from my house, pulled you beside me into the small body of icy water. Januaries have never been the same, and for years, nothing got in the way of our kissing, not our losses, not our gains.

If I saw you from across a crowded room—tall and bearded, with that glint in your eye—my heart would jolt, breath flutter, and when you'd see me and smile, my legs became reluctant to do their job, yet found their way to you. Our kisses came with us everywhere—to the corner store, the movie house, your mother's kitchen. They were our other way of talking. We'd bring our mouths together when everyone was looking and when no one was. Remember that time at Penn Station when I waited for you at the top of the escalator, how we began kissing before our lips even touched? One kiss could lead to another, and another to another, and later we'd sit down to dinner, half-dressed, still flushed and soft inside.

I miss wanting your mouth and the heft of your body, moving or still, naked beside mine. Old now, no longer lit by the passion we were sure would be undying, our attention is drawn by other things. Most days we peck each other's mouths like birds picking up seed. I miss the way a day could turn on our kissing, how it could make sparks flare hot inside, take fear away, lift sorrow.

Above the Crevasse

Kelp feathers
ebb and flow
phosphorescent
scales

Now I am raised up
the locked door and the silver
candelabra, the burnished years
spinning out

This is how we die

Trekkers, at earth's pinnacle,
cling to ice face
before the chill seeps in
at dusk

brushstroke
of clouds

Awakening

Dawn disburses dreams into sunrise, onrushing intellect
to greet what the waters have to teach us in the welcoming hues
of waking. Some days stay pillowed past noon, but most
beginnings lavish reds across Santa Monica and pyrotech
joy up the mountains ranging above Palm Springs.
Cumulus clouds loft glory everywhere: tumult above,
mirror-calm below. I hope for my childhood favorite,
the magical pattern of buttermilk skies, as if wings
had skiffed mist into down over the whole realm. By midday,
pure openness extends to the near edge of Catalina and behind,
out to sea, pulsing a watercolor blend of transcendent
atmosphere around Point Dume on the far side of the bay.
Oftentimes, enclosing the epic ocean in a languid bowl of light,
the marine layer unreels scrolls that define the horizon's curve.
Sunset flashes color wheel extremes: Expansive aquamarine
to royal blue parallels poppy red orange, swaying to starry night.

There's nothing subtle about winter at its peak
between sighing and awakening from the silence of sleep...

The faint strains of a dusky torch song flame
into spinning physics. Above Solstice Canyon,
my mind wheels toward you through watery traffic
in a blue zone of demystified rhythms—to reclaim
swift shadow sounds and tantalizing aromas. Oh yes.
I hunger for your warm vicinity heaped on bedclothes
enfolded by a bright time that still remembers our name.

Balboa

Before I understood luck, I played on the soft beaches of Balboa
Island, where I reluctantly learned to swim in a canal dotted with
small boats and private docks. My memory confides that there was
never a rainy day then and all the people were happy.

I was filled with innocence, wet sand in my belly. From the public
dock my drop line hung hopeful, a need for more, absent.

Our dwelling was a tiny rented house on Crystal Avenue, the beds of
four dreaming children gathered close. On Sundays our parents slept
late. My sister took her younger charges out early in the morn when
light spread across the easy water.

We gathered urchins and starfish, mussels, our prizes dragged home
on the bristles of a worn-out broom. They were laid on the roof to dry.
Apart from the stench was the cruelty.

On many weekends my sister pilfered change from our mother's
purse and took me on the ferry to the Fun Zone on Newport
Peninsula. The ferry was a nickel each and the sparkling water and
eager breeze at the gunwales was worth a million of those.

Sunday nights our family took to a small commercial craft,
plain but for its string of colored lights borrowed from a Christmas
tree. In the darkness and silence, we drifted with strangers, the voices
of a lazy evening whispering from patios just ashore.

There were many trips to Baja. A man with a knife once killed a bull
in front of us, and I remember a family with nine children, their lives
collected in a home of cardboard. We left them a polaroid picture of
themselves and an abundance of clothing we'd outgrown.

Long before we knew the suffering of all the world, our days were
honey-colored light.

Legacy

You don't want me to sell the store
where your dad worked for forty years;
it's your legacy, you say.
I was hoping to leave you more

than a building with four walls, lots of doors.
Hard to articulate what that would be, maybe
we'll call up the trivial in the coming years,
that weekend we gorged on oysters spawned

in Tomales Bay, together days, the Barcelona
trip, and what we called the holy days, the
every day days, quotidian details that became
some of our best memories. I grow old. Be kind

to each other; that's what I have to give. You'll
trash my piles of unread clippings, you'll split up
things, get some cash. Lucky sisters, you two, to
be two, and you have those kids. I leave you

plain love. You can see it clearly in that photograph,
the one Vanessa took on Christmas day, me with
my four grandkids lined up beind me in such a way,
they seem to be sprouting from my head.

I Go Out at Night to Breathe the Stars & Pray for Rain

After the song "California Stars" by Woody Guthrie

It's twilight and the great orange-peel sky
darkens to blueberry, blackberry, sweet
juice of night, Venus brightening
over distant water. I long
to lay my shoulder on the ragged bark
of an old live oak, breathe
the stars on the sage-salt wind.

Days of full sun, dry fields, thistle,
vinegar weed, they all came early.
Oak trees fell, cut off from water
by drought, dead from the root.
Sun gaped through the canopy.

I studied the plan to regrow the grove,
tied my shoelaces, lugged water,
found the protected seedlings,
chose one to be mine; it's number 599.

On the uphill road before the ruts turn
to crest the hill, I want to hold out my hand
to the wind, animal of little wetness.
I want to kneel in that silky cool dust.

White Noise

Unusual to hear the distant din
of the 101 freeway up here. It must be
the rush of holiday traffic
this Sunday afternoon before Christmas

in the quiet I've created,
pressing the off button
on my oxygen concentrator, a new friend,
sort of, I am tethered to day and night.

It whirs, beeps, clicks, pops, in combinations
of twos and threes, and underlying all that
is a persistent white noise,
enough to drive a person crazy,

a person who loves the quiet in the sound
of the many birds in the foothills
where we live. We are so lucky
they still thrive here and we get to feed
the little finches their favorite Niger seed.
A family of quail and a chipmunk or two gather
below the feeders to enjoy leftovers.

I'm reminded of my visit to the optometrist
the other day and the Visit Summary they emailed.
In a few places on the form, the doctor
described this or that facet of my eye health
as "calm and quiet." These words keep returning

—not in their intended context—
but rather as something I've been missing.
Like right now *calm and quiet,*
the oxygen concentrator off.

Scrappy

Not very long ago,
    you covered our family,
        warmed us against a freeze.
            intended our survival.

Rectangles, squares, and triangles,
    scraps, sourced and sorted,
        snipped from Grandpa's faded torn blue coveralls,
            Auntie May's lazy daisy precious print dress,
                Brother's favorite church-goin' shirt.

Neighbor ladies assembled like bees outside their hive,
    as you stretched taut over the quilting frame.

All the women stitched like symphony musicians,
    each her own conductor,
        made music with threaded needle.
            Pop! Down through the battin', then out the back.
           Cloth pieces, assembled, made whole.

Graduated,
    you're an art form now,
        your abstractness adorns walls,
           graces museum halls.

Legends

Kiss the lost shepherd
for his sheep lie sprawled
where his shadow looms
on the road dwarfed
by towering trees.

The leaves swirl around the hooves
like ghosts in olive, cinnamon, and sunset hues.
The seasons of love and loss,
both fragile and robust.

The moon no longer hides.
Its bold appearance
lays down the weight of burdens
hanging them off the crescent
until they blend into the night.

A reminder to harmonize with the wind,
find your voice and sing
about the days of your father,
discover your Hail Mary, your Hallelujah
in the love of second-grade paintings
taped to the refrigerator door.

Live your journey
of waves, sand castles,
found silver dollars,
and wayward jellyfish
in a universe of dreams
that has no bounds, only time
telling the story on parchment
written in the shoe polish
of a life well-lived.

Catalog

apply anti-itch cream on scar as if no one is looking, message from Dropbox that storage is full, jot down: *floating weeds, breakaway props,* worry about mom in hospital, doctor draining 1½ liters of fluid from her lungs, look up meaning of *shim* then *wild wall*, make turmeric ginger tea, search "pink vintage A-line dress," text friend who can't move from bed, buy dark chocolate sunflower butter cups, read about latest drive-by shooting, snip dead daisy petals, think of my students in Yangon unable to leave their homes, note number of white hairs falling on black sweater, remember found nest on last week's walk, write on back of envelope: *grief broke up visions of ourselves.*

Crows Tell My Fortune

My face is a mirror of the world.
Cracked mirror. Hungry mouth. An empty
kettle on the hearth. A clock ticking
out of sync with heartbeat. Usual
number of portals, apertures of
sound and light. What enters sickens me.
What emanates too often wounding.
There is no accounting for the crimes
of my face. Only the broken-winged songbird
of my regret. She no longer sings.
Her sky is empty, like my face. So
much time on the clock—when does it run out?
My eyes avoid my face in the mirror;
the world circumvents its crimes. Empty
kettle trills 'til its voice sputters out.

I was born to burn, feet on fire, limbs
wands or trees or candles or matchsticks,
the road goes up in flames, brain blazing.
No reason to camouflage; I miss
the colors my skin would turn, the wind
scorching my crust, crackle that escapes
the lips of those who no longer visit.
When no one visits, does the grave mourn?
Sometimes the universe is listening
and delivers what it thinks you want.
Tea leaf fortune tells not the future
but the past. Past I tried to forget.
Past where crows perch on the fence each morning
waiting for me. They never forget
my face. My face is a mirror of the world.

To Leonard from Virginia Woolf

Shall I put on my black dress
with cobweb arms?
Shall I wear shoes or no shoes?
Shall I walk, shall I run?
I've just dreamt of your shells
sinking soft into mud.
I shall wear my white slippers
and walk round my room
one last time, touching nothing
and wait for near darkness,
that quiet grey time
when I know what I must do
to silence the singing
the ringing the calling,
that dark heart red fear that propels me,
forgive me, I'm not quite myself
and these moments come rising so fast
I can't quell them.

I'm letting go, walking in,
see how these words to myself
help submerge the black spider,
I must be done with her.

I've loved you, I've held you,
You've loved me, you've held me,
forgive me, I'm walking in peace
to the river.

Sometimes in dreams
I can breathe in the ocean.
I hold my breath
And then suck in warm water.
I swim and kick
and finally I'm free.

On the short-term rental of our bodies:
A complaining tone of voice

The night removes our masks. Day attaches them to our faces yet doesn't give us even a shadow of a sword we can use in our own defense. This pisses me off. Meanwhile, our faces are either stone or wax. Our hearts are either steel or butter. We get smaller the farther away we go. The tragic, like a horse with blinders on, has lost its perspective. The sky, a solid block of invisible ink, shows us no signs, gives us no guidance. Sure, some of us have weightlifters in our brains doing the heavy lifting. Even they can't know they're forgetting something because in a flash, it's forgotten. A poet/fortune teller once told me: *in seed time, write; in harvest, write; in winter, write.* I said to her, in a complaining tone of voice: stars of exhaustion burst like bubbles around my consciousness! *Are you alive?* she said. *Then stop complaining.*

Sapphic Ode to Redwoods

At sunrise in another season of drought
under a lavish canopy of redwoods,
the fog water drips down into thirsty roots
in the forest floor.

The coastal amazons of the woodland, their
leafy crowns stretch toward sky reaching for stars,
bark shields barely scorched by wildfire fingers
at breasts of heartwood.

Legacy of their long-lived mystery,
circled by pristine fairy rings of fresh growth,
warriors battle against being toppled
by the wrath of wind.

Lisa Alvarez's poetry and prose have appeared in journals including *About Place Journal, Air/Light, Anacapa Review, Huizache,* and *Santa Monica Review,* and in several anthologies. A professor of English at Irvine Valley College, in the summers, she co-directs Writing Workshops at the Community of Writers. Her debut collection, *Some Final Beauty and other Stories,* is forthcoming in 2025 from the University of Nevada Press.

Lori Anaya, poet, teacher, writer, and Macondista, received her M.S. in bilingual Special Education from Cal Lutheran University, Thousand Oaks, and her bilingual K-12 teaching credential from the University of California, Santa Barbara. She is a South Coast Writing Project Fellow with work published in short story and poetry literary magazines and in *Out of the Ground: Poems Inspired by Santa Barbara Botanic Garden* (Gunpowder Press). When not writing, she rides a paint mare into a central coastal land preserve where nature overlooks the fact that she is human.

Cynthia Anderson has published 13 poetry collections, most recently *The Far Mountain* (Wise Owl Publications), *Arrival* (Sheila-Na-Gig Editions), and *Full Circle* (Cholla Needles Press). Her poems appear frequently in journals and anthologies, and her work has been nominated for the Pushcart Prize and Best of the Net. Anderson is co-editor of the anthology, *A Bird Black As the Sun: California Poets on Crows & Ravens.* She has lived in California for over 40 years.

Joan Annsfire is a retired librarian who lives in Berkeley. Her poetry chapbook, *Distant Music* was published by Headmistress Press. Her poems have appeared in anthologies including *Wild Crone Wisdom; 11/9: The Fall of American Democracy; The Times They Were A-Changing, Women Remember the 60's and 70's; The Queer Collection; Milk and Honey,* and *The Other Side of the Postca*rd, and in journals such as *Sinister Wisdom, Rising Phoenix Review, Birdland Journal, Older Queer Women: The Intimacy of Survival, Poet's Basement, Lavender Review, The 13th Moon,* and others.

Debby Arrin is a retired small business owner who spends these days taking care of grandchildren, reading everything she can get her hands on, and writing poetry, creative non-fiction, and essays.

Virginia Barrett is a poet, writer, artist, editor, and educator. She earned her MFA in Writing from the University of San Francisco where she was poetry editor of *Switchback.* Her six books of poetry include *Between Looking* and *Crossing Haight—San Francisco poems.* She is also the editor of four poetry anthologies including *RED: a Hue Are You anthology.*

Ellen Bass's most recent book is *Indigo* (Copper Canyon). Among her awards are Fellowships from the Guggenheim Foundation, NEA, Lambda Literary Award, and four Pushcart Prizes. With Florence Howe, she co-edited the first major anthology of women's poetry, *No More Masks!* (Doubleday, 1973), and she co-authored the groundbreaking *The Courage to Heal: A Guide for Survivors of Child Sexual Abuse*. A Chancellor Emerita of the Academy of American Poets, Bass founded poetry workshops at Salinas Valley State Prison and Santa Cruz jails. She teaches in Pacific University's MFA program and online *Living Room Craft Talks*.

Amy Bates is a poet, living and working in San Francisco, California. She is a graduate of Whitman College, with a BA in English Literature. Married for 47 years to a painter who was struck down with profound dementia, she uses her new solitude to write; to create a new identity. Her main foci are sex, love, death, loss, and scenes glimpsed in passing from the windows of a bus.

Donna Becker is a poet, retired family law attorney and sometimes botanical artist. She lived for 40 years in Santa Cruz County. She now lives in the Sierra Foothills where she is deeply touched by the rugged and beautiful California landscape. Her work has been published in *Porter Gulch Review; Phren-Z, An Online Literary Magazine for Santa Cruz County; Out of the Fire, A Calaveras Anthology; Calaveras Poets and Community Poems*; and *First Women in Yale College: Reflections on Coeducation for the 50th Anniversary Celebration*. She was honored to read at In Celebration of the Muse in Santa Cruz County.

Laurel Benjamin is a San Francisco Bay Area poet, active with the Women's Poetry Salon. She curates Ekphrastic Writers and is a reader for *Common Ground Review*. Her publications include: *Pirene's Fountain, Lily Poetry Review, Cider Press Review, Taos Journal of Poetry, Mom Egg Review, Gone Lawn,* and *Nixes Mate*. She is a *Cider Press Review* Book Award finalist, Pushcart Prize nominee, and received an Honorable Mention for the Ruben Rose Memorial Poetry Competition. Laurel holds an MFA from Mills College. She invented a secret language with her brother.

Cynthia Bernard is in her early seventies, a long-time classroom teacher and an emerging writer of poetry, short fiction, and creative nonfiction. She lives and writes on a hill overlooking the ocean, about 25 miles south of San Francisco. Her work has appeared in *Multiplicity Magazine, Passager, Verse-Virtual, Poetry Breakfast, The Seattle Star*, and elsewhere. She was selected by Western Rivers Conservancy to serve as the Poet-Protector of Deer Creek Falls in the northern Sierra Nevada foothills.

Emily Bernhardt, retired from Glendale and Accountancy, lives in Ventura, California, where she explores the natural world, craft projects and writing poetry.

Les Bernstein is an award-winning poet and anthologist whose poems have appeared in journals and anthologies in the United States and internationally. Her full-length book *Loose Magic* was reviewed by the *Los Angeles Review of Books* and is available on Amazon.

Doreen Beyer is a recently-retired school nurse enjoying her second life reading and writing poetry. Poetry starts with a good impulse; for her that impulse was the birth of her first grandchild in July 2023. She lives with her husband and little brown dog in Sacramento.

Kim Birdsong was born and adopted in Naples, Italy, and has lived most of her life on the Monterey Peninsula. She is a counselor, an artist, author and photographer. Birdsong spent 16 years working with survivors of sexual assault and trauma. She hosted a radio show, "Spirit Matters." She recently published her first volume of poetry, *Rain to Root: poems of meeting grief and grace.* She has a small, private counseling practice and facilitates grief workshops and rituals.

Sheryl J. Bize-Boutte is the author of the historical fiction novels, *Betrayal on the Bay*ou, and *Back to the Bayou: The Tassin Valley Saga Continues.* Her work has appeared in *Harlequin, Hanover Press, Read Carpet Magazine* (Columbia), *The East Bay Times, Newa American Dabu* (India), *NPR's Bay Poets, Writers Digest* and elsewhere. She is also a teacher, presenter, curator, panelist, moderator and speaker for writing and literary events, and is the 2026 Poetry Track Coordinator for San Francisco Writers Conference.

Lisa Black, born in North Hollywood, has lived much of her life in Southern California. For decades she acted in plays and created original performances as a solo artist and in ensembles. Recently, her short fiction has appeared in *Santa Monica Review* and *Citric Acid.* Her sound poetry and spoken word pieces have been broadcast via *SoundPedro*, Space Cowboy Books' *Simultaneous Times* Podcast, and in an ongoing musical collaboration as Black Masheeen.

Amrita Skye Blaine has been writing poetry steadily since she turned 70. For the last three years, she has written a poem every morning. Her poems have been published by *Braided Way Magazine, The Penwood Review, Delta Poetry Review, New English Review, Soul Forte* and *Amethyst Review.* Her first book *strange grace: the ending season* features poems on impermanence and aging, *every riven thing* is new from Finishing Line Press.

Lavina Blossom grew up in rural Michigan and now lives in Southern California. She has written articles on the writing process for the Inlandia Institute and was a poetry editor for Inlandia's online journal. Her poems have appeared in various publications, including *3Elements Review, The Paris Review, Poemeleon, Common*

Ground Review, Gyroscope Review, and *Ekphrastic Review*. Two flash stories are forthcoming in *Okay Donkey*.

Laure-Anne Bosselaar is the author of *The Hour Between Dog and Wolf, Small Gods of Grief*, winner of the Isabella Gardner Prize, and of *A New Hunger*, an ALA Notable Book, and *These Many Rooms*. Her most recent book is *Lately: New & Selected Poems* (Sungold Editions). The editor of five anthologies, and the recipient of a Pushcart Prize, she served as Santa Barbara's Poet Laureate from 2019 to 2021.

Beverly Boyd taught literature and writing in Southern California before retiring to the Central Coast. For more than ten years, she has curated a quarterly poetry reading series at a local library. Her poems appear in *American Journal of Nursing, Healing Muse, Miramar, Poem, Slant, Slipstream,* and others. Her work is also included in *Voices from the Porch* (Main Street Rag), *Corners of the Mouth* (DeerTree Press), and *Still You* (Wolf Ridge Press). She is co-author of *Where Our Palms Rest* (Coalesce Press) with poets Carol Alma McPhee, Joann Rusch, and Bonnie Young.

Susan Brandes is a fifth-generation Californian living in Santa Cruz County. After retiring from a 36-year career as an electrical engineer she had the great fortune of touring with the Cabrillo Symphonic Chorus first to Cuba and then to South Africa where they sang in the townships. Though she has always had a love of poetry, it has only been in her later adulthood that she has endeavored to create poems. She recently completed her MFA at Pacific University and is now working on submitting her work to journals.

Lynne Bronstein is the author of *Nasty Girls* (Four Feathers Press) and four other books of poetry. She has been published in magazines ranging from *Playgirl* to *Chiron Review,* from *Lummox* to anthologies in England, Ireland, Canada, and India. Her short fiction has appeared in magazines and anthologies and has been read on National Public Radio. She also writes a column called *Show Biz Cats*.

M. L. Brown is the author of *Call It Mist*, winner of the Three Mile Harbor Press Book Prize, and *Drought*, winner of the Claudia Emerson Chapbook award. Her work has appeared in *Valparaiso Poetry Review, Prairie Schooner*, and *Cave Wall*, among other journals and anthologies including, *Blue Will Rise Over Yellow: An International Poetry Anthology for Ukraine*.

Susan Browne is the author of *Buddha's Dogs, Zephyr*, and *Just Living*. Her poetry collection, *Monster Mash*, is forthcoming from Four Way Books in 2025. Awards include prizes from Four Way Books, the Catamaran Poetry Prize and the James Dickey Poetry Prize.

Martha Browning, born in Jackson, Michigan, has lived in Los Angeles for most of her life. Martha has a degree in English literature from UCLA. She is a mother and grandmother and currently resides in Westchester with her husband.

Julie Bruck is from Montreal and has lived in San Francisco since 1997. Her most recent collection is *How to Avoid Huge Ships* (Brick Books). Her poems have appeared in *Plume, The New Yorker, Poetry Daily,* and *The Academy of American Poets' Poem-A-Day*, among other venues. Her third book, *Monkey Ranch* (Brick Books), won Canada's 2012 Governor General's Literary Award for poetry, and *How to Avoid Huge Ships* was a finalist for the same award in 2019. She has just finished a new book manuscript, *We Love You Get Up.*

Valerie Anne Burns has had essays published from her book, *Caution: Mermaid Crossing, Voyages of a Motherless Daughter* in *Sad Girl Diaries, Grande Dame Literary, Sea to Sky Review, The Remnant Archive, HerStry, Chicken Soup for the Soul: Tough Times Won't Last but Tough People Will* and *Rituals Anthology*. In September 2021, she received a finalist award for her manuscript from Page Turner Awards. Additionally, she's created a workshop called "Living and Healing Through Color" that's presented to women survivors at retreats overseas. Valerie Anne is a breast cancer survivor living in Santa Barbara with her therapy cat, Lucia.

Elena Karina Byrne is a former Kingsley & Kate Tufts Poetry Awards judge. She works as a freelance editor and professor, Programming Consultant & Poetry Stage Manager for *The Los Angeles Times* Festival of Books. Pushcart Prize and Best American Poetry recipient, Elena's five poetry collections *include If This Makes You Nervous* (Omnidawn Publishing). Currently, Elena is writing screenplays while completing her collection of essays entitled *Voyeur Hour: Poetry, Art, Film, and Desire.*

Mary Camarillo is the author of two award-winning novels: *Those People Behind Us* and *The Lockhart Women*. Her poems and short fiction have appeared in publications and anthologies such as the *California Writer's Club Literary Anthology, Inlandia, 166 Palms, The Ear,* and the *Sonora Review*. Camarillo lives in Huntington Beach, California, with her husband who plays ukulele and their terrorist cat, Riley, who makes frequent appearances on Instagram.

Jina Carvalho was born and raised in rural Portugal, before immigrating to Canada in 1958. She has degrees in Psychology and the Performing Arts. Jina has performed in theater, spoken word and dance productions throughout Canada and the US. Her first poetry collection *The Weight of Desire: A Poetry Memoir* was published by Sungold Editions. Carvalho is currently working on a book about the experience of caring for her husband until his recent death. For the past 45 years, she has been involved in the mental health nonprofit sector.

Susan Chiavelli is the recipient of the *Chattahoochee Review*'s Lamar York Nonfiction Prize for "Death, Another Country," also named a notable essay by *Best American Essays*. Her award-winning prose and poetry have appeared in *The Los Angeles Review, SALT, Miramar*, several Shoreline Voices anthologies and elsewhere. Susan was born and raised in Seattle and now lives on the edge of Rattlesnake Canyon in Santa Barbara.

Carolyn Chilton Casas has lived most of her life on the central coast of California, the perfect landscape for a love of hiking and playing beach volleyball. Her poetry has been published in journals such as *Braided Way, Grateful Living, ONE ART, The Mindful Word*, and *Third Wednesday*, and in anthologies including *Out of the Ground and The Wonder of Small Things: Poems of Peace and Renewal*. More of Carolyn's work can be found on Facebook or Instagram and in her newest collection of poetry, *Under the Same Sky*.

Sally Churgel is a poet, healer/intuitive, transformation guide and Argentine tango dancer. She was poet laureate of Congregation Ner Shalom from 2009-2019 and is published in their anthology *In the Light of Peace*. Her healing business, Call to Joy, teaches that "your life is poetry, your body the words. When out of sorts, life may feel like a stale poem." Sally lives in Northern California with her husband whom she met and married after age 62.

Susan Cohen is a Berkeley poet and translator and the author of three collections: *Throat Singing* (Cherry Grove Collections), *A Different Wakeful Animal* (Red Dragonfly Press), and *Democracy of Fire* (Broadstone Books). Her poetry has appeared in *32 Poems, Anacapa Review, Prairie Schooner, Rattle, Southern Review* and *Verse Daily*, and she has received the Red Wheelbarrow Prize, Terrain Annual Poetry Prize, and a Pushcart Special Mention, among other honors.

Jean Colonomos began her career in the arts as a member of the Martha Graham Dance Company in NYC in the 1960s. She segued into writing dance journalism, plays, and poems. An award-winner in all three genres, her work has appeared online and in poetry journals. Her chapbook is *Art Farm* (Finishing Line Press). Her full-length volume, *Living the Dream* (Kelsay Books), is available on Amazon.

Marie Connors, 74, after a decade working as a writer and editor for print and media in Memphis, Tennessee, relocated to Southern California in 1986. She earned an MFA in English from UC Irvine, and has published in literary journals including *Faultline, South Coast Poetry Review, The Ear*, and in the anthology, *Orange County: A Literary Field Guide*. Her short lyric poetry aspires to reimagine everyday experiences as a mythic journey in search of a common humanity.

Ann Conradsen has been writing and appearing in readings for many years in San Francisco and Sacramento. She received an MA in English (Concentration

Creative Writing) from San Francisco State University, where she studied with Stan Rice, Frances Mayes, Frances Phillips, and Kathleen Fraser. Her work has appeared in *Laurel Review, Plainsongs* and in *The Sacramento Anthology: 100 Poems*. She lives in Sacramento where she spends many hours at the river.

Susan Read Cronin, best known for her bronze allegorical and humorous sculptures, is the author of *Bronze Casting in a Nutshell*. She spent most of her adult life in Vermont and since moving to Santa Barbara has focused on poetry. She has published three books of poetry: *Notices, OPEN* and *What's Left*.

Pamela Davis, a career writer, is the author of *Lunette*, winner of the ABZ Poetry Book Award in 2015. She has two Pushcart Poetry Prize nominations, was finalist for the *American Literary Review* Poetry Prize, and has twice been a finalist for the Pablo Neruda Poetry Award from *Nimrod Journal*. Publication credits include poems in *Cimarron Review, New Ohio Review, Prairie Schooner, Smartish Pace*, and others. Born in Long Beach, California, she lives in Santa Barbara and is finalizing her second book of poems.

Fran Davis is an essayist and poet whose work has been published in the *L.A. Times, New Verse News, Calyx, The Chattahoochee Review, The Vincent Brothers Review, Reed Magazine, Passager, The Hopper*, and several anthologies. She is a winner of the Lamar York prize York prize for nonfiction and a Pushcart Prize nominee.

Carol V. Davis is the author of *Below Zero, Because I Cannot Leave This Body* and *Between Storms*. She won the 2007 T.S. Eliot Prize for *Into the Arms of Pushkin: Poems of St. Petersburg*. Her poetry has been read on National Public Radio, the Library of Congress, and Radio Russia. Twice a Fulbright scholar in Russia, she taught in Siberia in 2018 and now teaches in Los Angeles. Donna Sternberg and Dancers is using Davis' poetry in the recent piece, "Ancestors' Voices."

Lucille Lang Day has published four poetry chapbooks and seven full-length collections, most recently *Birds of San Pancho and Other Poems of Place*. She is also the editor of *Poetry and Science: Writing Our Way to Discovery*, coeditor of *Fire and Rain: Ecopoetry of California* and *Red Indian Road West: Native American Poetry from California*, and author of two children's books and a memoir. Her many honors include the Blue Light Poetry Prize, two PEN Oakland – Josephine Miles Literary Awards, the Joseph Henry Jackson Award, and eleven Pushcart nominations. She is founder and publisher of Scarlet Tanager Books.

Marsha de la O is a lecturer in the English Department at CSU Channel Islands, where she teaches poetry and creative writing. She is the author of *Every Ravening Thing, Antidote for Night*, and *Black Hope*. Her poems have appeared in *The New*

Yorker, The Slowdown, and many journals, and she is a recipient of the Morton Marcus Poetry Prize. She lives with her husband in Ventura, where they founded the Ventura County Poetry Project to support local poetry.

Carol Dorf has received fellowships from the Hawthornden Foundation, Zoeglossia, and the Napa Valley Writers' Conference. Their writing appears on the Poetry Foundation website, in several chapbooks, and in journals including *Pleiades, About Place, Cutthroat, Braving the Body*, among others. Founding poetry editor of *Talking Writing*, they taught math and writing in Berkeley USD, as well as at museums and conferences.

Rebecca Dougherty is a sixth-generation Californian whose relatives headed west during the Gold Rush. Living in the Sacramento Valley, she has been involved in agriculture her entire life. She also has graduate degrees in education and technology. Now that she has retired from teaching, she belongs to the No Fear poetry group. Her poems have been published in *Volume Poetry*.

Lynn Downey is a native California writer, historian, and archivist. Her work is centered in the West, where her family has lived for over a century, and she has written about the history of women's health, the culture of the dude ranch, and the life of Levi Strauss, after 25 years as the company Historian for Levi Strauss & Co. in San Francisco. She grew up in Marin and Sonoma counties, and now lives in the town of Sonoma, where she grows Pinot Noir grapes in her backyard and occasionally makes wine.

Terri Drake is a graduate of the Iowa Writers' Workshop. Her poetry chapbook *Regarding Us* was published in 2023. Her poetry collection, *At the Seams* was published by Bear Star Press. Her poems have appeared in *The Chicago Quarterly Review, Crab Creek Review, Poets Reading the News,* and *Open: Journal of Art and Letters,* among others. A practicing psychoanalyst, she lives in Santa Cruz.

Kimbrough Ernest teaches with California Poets in the Schools in Ventura and Santa Barbara Counties. She has been published in several anthologies and, in 2024, won prizes in both the Ventura and Santa Barbara Poetry Festivals.

Alexis Rhone Fancher is a poet/photographer who is published in *Best American Poetry, Rattle, The American Journal of Poetry, Spillway*, and elsewhere. Her photos are published worldwide. She's authored 10 poetry collections, most recently, *Triggered*, (MacQueens) and *Brazen* (NYQ). A coffee table book of over 100 of Alexis' photographs of Southern California poets is published by Moon Tide Press. She calls the Mojave Desert home.

Laurel Feigenbaum was born and raised in California. She credits her interest in poetry to Wordsworth and her father who loved word play. After careers in education and business, she began writing in her 80s. Matriarch of her family now, she is the mother of three, grandmother of seven, and great-grandmother of eight. Her work can be found in *The Amsterdam Quarterly* and *The Marin Poetry Center Anthology*, as well as her recent book *Life In No Ordinary Time.*

Molly Fisk writes poetry and radio commentary from the Sierra foothills. Her most recent book of poems is *The More Difficult Beauty*; her latest commentary is *Everything But the Kitchen Skunk*. She edited *California Fire & Water, A Climate Crisis Anthology*, with a Poets Laureate Fellowship from the Academy of American Poets. She's received grants from the National Endowment for the Arts and the Corporation for Public Broadcasting. *Walking Wheel,* her collection of linked historical poems, is forthcoming from Red Hen Press.

Rebecca Foust's most recent books are *You Are Leaving the American Sector: Love Poems* (Backbone Press) and *Only* (Four Way Books, starred review in Publisher's Weekly). Her poems have in recent years won the James Dickey, Fischer, *New Ohio Review*, Pablo Neruda, James Hearst, and *Poetry International* prizes. Other recognitions include fellowships from The Frost Place, Hedgebrook, MacDowell, and Sewanee, and a Marin County Poet Laureateship where her program, "Poetry as Sanctuary," featured readings by local immigrant poets.

Nancy Fowler's writing asserts that acknowledgement of a specific person, place or action is an initial step in understanding, respect and love. Her work has been previously published in *Tidepools, Gemini, Songs of the San Joaquin, Naugatauk River Review,* and other literary journals. In Washington State, her work has appeared on posters for Bainbridge Island's Poetry Corners event and has thrice been included in the Port Angeles Fine Arts Center's Poetry in the Park Program, with yearlong displays in the Webster Woods Sculpture Park.

Diane Funston has been published in *Lake Affect Magazine, Synkronicity, Still Points Quarterly* and many others. Her chapbook *Over the Falls* was published by Foothills Publishing. Funston is on the spectrum of neurodiversity and her personality type, INFJ, is the rarest in the world. She lives in Marysville, California, an old gold rush small town outside of Sacramento. She shares her life with her husband and three loving rescue dogs.

Catherine Gewertz has been a garage band singer, pie baker, cocktail waitress and newspaper reporter. She's an inaugural member of Pride Poets, a troupe of queer poets who compose on-demand poems for strangers on the streets of Los Angeles, using vintage typewriters. Catherine is a graduate of Stanford University. Her work appears in *Rogue Agent, Quartet, Stone Poetry Quarterly,* and *Raw Art Review*, among others.

Delores Gilmore is a student of poetry writing, a lifelong Californian, and a beach enthusiast. She's President of Zonta Club South Bay a 501(c)(3) charitable organization. She is a retired Vice President of Human Resources in the fashion/apparel, manufacturing and retail industries. She holds degrees in Business, from California Pacific University, and Advanced HR Studies, from UCLA.

Terri Glass lives among redwood and black bear near Crescent City. A writer of essay, poetry and haiku, her work has appeared in journals including *Eastern Iowa Review, Fourth River, About Place, California Quarterly*, and many anthologies, including *Wild Gods, Fire and Rain: Ecopoetry of California*, and *Earth Blessings*. Her recent books include *Being Animal* (Kelsay Books), a chapbook of haiku: *Birds, Bees, Trees, Love, Hee Hee* (Finishing Line Press). She is a longtime teacher and former Program Director of CAL POETS in the Schools.

Valentina Gnup's first poetry collection is *Ruined Music* (Grayson Books). She has been awarded the Tucson Festival of Books Literary Award for Poetry, the Lascaux Prize in Poetry, the Ekphrastic Challenge from *Rattle*, the *Rattle* Reader's Choice Award, the Barbara Mandigo Kelly Peace Poetry Award from the Nuclear Age Peace Foundation, and the Joy Harjo Poetry Award from *Cutthroat Journal of the Arts*. A native Californian, she currently lives in Oakland.

D. R. Goodman is the author of *Greed: A Confession* (Able Muse Press). Twice winner of the Able Muse Write Prize for poetry and winner of the Howard Nemerov Sonnet Award, her work has appeared in the *New Ohio Review, THINK Journal, Whitefish Review, Crazyhorse*, and many others, as well as in Ted Kooser's *American Life in Poetry, Extreme Sonnets* (Beth Houston, editor) and *150 Contemporary Sonnets* (William Baer, editor). A native of Oak Ridge, Tennessee, she is a long-time resident of Oakland, where she is founder and chief instructor at a martial arts school.

Caroline Goodwin's recent books are *Old Snow, White Sun* (JackLeg Press), *Madrigals* (Big Yes Press) and *Matanuska* (Aquifer Press, Wales, UK). A former Stegner fellow in poetry at Stanford, she lives and teaches in the San Francisco Bay Area.

Celeste Goyer is a poet and visual artist living in Los Angeles. Her debut collection is *The Shoes of Our Guests* (Giant Claw). She edited a literary quarterly for 14 years. Her poems have appeared in *Aperçus, Times Times 3*, and *The Columbia Review*, among others. She is a member of the Wild Orchid Collective, an interdisciplinary literary and visual arts group based in Venice, California. Born in Northampton, Massachusetts, she has lived in California since age 11, mostly in remote towns of the Mojave and Great Basin deserts.

Arabella Grayson professionally modeled in her 20s and 30s, and still acts. She looks at aging through the lens of commerce and the fragility of one's identity with longevity. Her poems appear in *We've Got Some Things to Say, 146 Poems of Love, Peregrine Journal, Poets Basement/Counterpunch.com, Mills Quarterly,* and elsewhere. She is a California native and former Santa Fe Art Institute writer-in-residence and Hurston/Wright Writer's Week alum.

Tammy Greenwood is a poet, printmaker, and Louisiana native residing in California. Her work is heavily influenced by the varying landscape and culture of the states she calls home. She is a Pushcart Prize nominee and her work appears or is forthcoming in *Rattle, Pinch, McNeese Review, Whale Road Review, SWWIM, Door is a Jar,* and elsewhere.

Susan Gubernat's most recent collection, *The Zoo at Night,* won the Raz-Shumaker Prize for a book of poetry and was published by the University of Nebraska Press. Individual poems have appeared in *Cimarron Review, Gargoyle, The Hudson Review, The Michigan Quarterly*, and other publications. An opera librettist and professor emerita in the English Department of California State University, East Bay, she lives in San Francisco.

Kathleen Gunton is a writer/photographer born and raised in California. After leaving the convent, she received her degree from CSULB. Her words and images appear in dozens of publications, including *CQ, Ellipsis, Gold Man Review, Rhino,* and *Thema*. Her most recent collection of poems is *Putting Words Next To Silence*. Though mother, grandmother, and great grandmother, she continues to give birth to new poems.

Joell Hallowell is a fourth-generation Californian who grew up in the foothills of the San Joaquin Valley and has lived in San Francisco since 1976, where she makes little oddball films, collects oral histories, edits and proofreads other people's writing, and tries her hand at fiction and poetry when life allows.

Stephanie Barbé Hammer is a seven-time Pushcart Prize nominee in fiction, nonfiction and poetry. Her writing has appeared in numerous literary journals; she has published two novels, one novella, one novelette, three poetry collections, three scholarly books, and a guidebook to writing magical realism. Hammer is a Professor Emerita in Comparative Literature at the University of California, Riverside, and she teaches creative writing at Hugo House, the Inlandia Institute, and the Santa Barbara Writers Conference.

Jan Hanson is a human resources director and author of the chapbook *I'll Never Play the Hammered Dulcimer* (Finishing Line Press). She enjoys reflecting her work life in her poetry, along with other aspects of her life and history. Her work has recently appeared in *LAdige, Quartet* and *The Healing Muse*. She lives with her husband in southern California, where in addition to working full-time in HR, she writes, hangs out with her granddaughters, and sings alto in a quartet.

Dianna Henning taught through California Poets in the Schools, received several California Arts Council grants, and taught poetry workshops through the William James Association's Prison Arts Program, including Folsom Prison. She runs The Thompson Peak Writers' Workshop. Publications credits include *One Art Poetry, Mocking Heart Review*, and *Worth More Standing, Poets and Activists Pay Homage to Trees*, among others. She's received seven Pushcart Prize nominations. She holds an MFA in Writing from Vermont College.

Leslie Hodge has poems published in *Catamaran Literary Reader, The Main Street Rag, South Florida Poetry Journal, ONE ART, Whale Road Review*, and elsewhere. Her chapbook, *Escape and other poems*, was published by Kelsay Books in 2024. Leslie is currently reading for *The Adroit Journal*. She lives in San Diego.

Catherine Abbey Hodges won the Barry Spacks Poetry Prize from Gunpowder Press for her book *Instead of Sadness*. She is and the author of three other full-length collections, most recently *Empty Me Full* (Gunpowder Press). Individual poems appear in venues including *Narrative, Plume, CALYX, Plant-Human Quarterly, SALT, Verse Daily* and *The Writer's Almanac*. English Professor Emeritus at Porterville College and nominee for the Pushcart Prize and Best of the Net, Catherine writes, edits, teaches privately, and collaborates with musician Rob Hodges on ancestral Yokuts land.

Karen Lee Hones is a San Francisco poet who has published in many literary journals, most recently in *The MacGuffin, Passager*, and *Bluff & Vine*. She's also published online in the San Francisco Public Library's "poem of the day" series. She has published two chapbooks of poetry: *Behind Dark Glasses* and *Lucy and Ricky*. After retiring from paid work, she is enjoying her creative life and her interest in birth and death doula activities. She also recently celebrated 15 years of continuous sobriety.

Elizabeth Iannaci is a partially sighted SoCal-based poet who earned her MFA in Poetry from VCFA. Widely published and anthologized, her latest chapbook is *The Virgin Turtle Light Show* (Latitude 34 Press). Recently, her poetry appeared in *Does It Have Pockets?, Interlitq, Hole in the Head Review, Pratik,* and the *San Diego Annual*. She has appeared at countless venues in the U.S. and Europe, has one son, three grandchildren, two grand pups, and prefers paisley to polka dots.

Johanna Jenkins moved to California from Washington State in 1988. She has a Master's Degree in Social Work. She has been writing poetry all her life, and in her 60's, she decided to begin studying it as a craft and a calling. She is now 84 and still practices as a therapist. This is her first publication.

Bonnie S. Kaplan is a multidisciplinary literary and performance artist with an MFA from California College of the Arts. Her poetry has appeared in *Sinister Wisdom, Room Magazine, TAB Journal,* and in numerous anthologies. Her manuscript *Where I Live Now* was a semifinalist in the Smith College Chapbook Contest, in collaboration with Nine Syllables Press. She grew up in the San Fernando Valley and still occasionally rides her beloved 70s skateboard.

Bonnilee Kaufman is on the cusp of 70; whatever it is 'they' say about older single lezbians is and isn't true. A Lambda Lit Fellow & QueerWise emeritus, she has presented poetry to audiences at Akbar on Sunset Boulevard; Women's Jazz Festival Palm Springs; CIRCA '23 Sapphic Voices & CIRCA '24 Succulent Senior Lesbians; and OUTWRITE DC '23 & '24. Highlighted in Feminist Center For Creative Work Oct '24, she contributes book reviews to *The Journal of Lesbian Studies.*

Lorelei Kay is the author of an award-winning memoir, *From Mormon to Mermaid—One Woman's Voyage from Oppression to Freedom.* She became hooked on poetry when her dad sat her down and helped her write her first poem. Her poems have since appeared in anthologies, online publications, and magazines. She has served as a poetry judge for the *California Writers Club Literary Review,* as a mentor on the Dorothy C. Blakely Memoir Project, and on the board of the High Desert Branch of The California Writers Club.

Peggy Kelly is a teacher, writer, and poet. She is a fellow of the South Coast Writing Project, a Crystal Apple Educator Award recipient, and the author of *Peg's Picks*, a weekly email newsletter for teachers. Her work has appeared in *California English, Out of the Ground: Poems Inspired by Santa Barbara Botanic Garden*, and other publications.

Susan Kelly-DeWitt is a former Wallace Stegner Fellow. Her books include *Frangible Operas* (Gunpowder Press), *Gatherer's Alphabet* (Gunpowder Press, California Poets Series), *Gravitational Tug* (Main Street Rag), *Spider Season* (Cold River Press), *The Fortunate Islands* (Marick Press) and a number of online and small press collections. Her work is widely anthologized and published in print and online journals at home and abroad.

Ellen Girardeau Kempler's poems have appeared in *The Dewdrop, Wild Roof Magazine, One Jacar Press, Tiny Seed Literary Journal,* and others. In 2024, her poem was shortlisted for The Bridgport Prize in Poetry. She won Ireland's Blackwater International Poetry Prize and honorable mention in Winning

Writers' Tom Howard/Margaret Reid Poetry Contest. Her chapbooks are *Thirty Views of a Changing World: Haiku + Photos* (Finishing Line) and *Fire in My Head / Flame in My Heart: Poems for the Pyrocene* (forthcoming from Kelsay Books).

Teri Ketchie is a former bilingual teacher and mentor in Watsonville. She writes poetry, plays guitar, and volunteers as a docent at a local wetland. Her poems, which weave together themes of nature, travel and family, have been published in *Tiny Seed Journal* and *The Nature of Our Times*. She was a featured reader at the 2024 and 2025 Santa Cruz Celebration of the Muse.

Joyce Kiefer grew up and raised her family in the San Francisco Bay Area. She attended San Jose State and worked for years in administration at Stanford. She's done numerous interviews for the oral history project of the Stanford Historical Society. Her short stories, poems, and creative nonfiction have appeared in various anthologies and in San Jose's *Mercury News*. She also writes a blog about her travels and discoveries in everyday life

Blair Kilpatrick is a psychologist whose life was transformed by a chance encounter with the Cajun accordion. She is the author of the music memoir *Accordion Dreams* (U. Press Mississippi) and received the first annual SUA literary award for her creative nonfiction. Her poetry has appeared in *ONE ART, MockingHeart Review, littledeathlit, Amethyst Review*, and elsewhere. She lives in Berkeley, where she plays in a Cajun band with her fiddler husband.

Veronica Kornberg is a poet from the Central Coast of California. Recipient of the Morton Marcus Poetry Prize, her work has appeared or is forthcoming in numerous journals, including *Alaska Quarterly Review, New Ohio Review, Poet Lore, Rattle,* and elsewhere. Veronica is a Peer Reviewer for *Whale Road Review*, an avid explorer of tidepools, and a habitat gardener.

Jennifer Lagier lives a block from the Monterey stage where Janis Joplin performed and Jimi Hendrix torched his guitar. Both of her parents were California natives. Jennifer grew up in the Central Valley but has lived on the Monterey Peninsula since 1987. She has published 23 books. Her work appears in a variety of anthologies and literary magazines. She taught with California Poets in the Schools, currently edits the *Monterey Poetry Review*, serves as Web Goddess for *Misfit Magazine*, and helps publicize Monterey Bay Poetry Consortium Second Saturday readings.

Sharon Langley writes and reads with Women Who Submit-Los Angeles. She is also a children's book author. *A Ride to Remember,* co-authored with Amy Nathan, illustrated by Floyd Cooper, tells the story of Gwynn Oak Amusement Park and her family's contribution to the park's integration. She is an educational consultant providing professional development in early literacy, culturally-relevant literature, and equity in gifted education. She is a graduate of Clark Atlanta University and Mount Saint Mary's University. She lives in Los Angeles.

Sheree La Puma is a writer and recent cancer survivor whose work has appeared in or is forthcoming in *Lake Effect: An International Literary Journal, The Penn Review, Redivider, Sugar House Review*, and *Catamaran Literary Reader*, among others. She earned her MFA in writing from CalArts. Her poetry has been nominated for *Best of The Net* and four Pushcarts. A reader for the *Orange Blossom Review*, her latest chapbook, *Broken: Do Not Use,* is currently available at Main Street Rag Publishing.

Diane Lefer's most recent novels feature scientists in the Mojave Desert who become terrorism suspects (*Out of Place*) and LA Zoo baboons with broken hearts (*Confessions of a Carnivore).* She has authored three books of stories, including *California Transit* which received the Mary McCarthy Prize. She has worked with asylum-seekers in L.A. and Tijuana, men on parole, youth affected by the criminal in/justice system, and vulnerable children in Colombia and Bolivia. She lives in Los Angeles with a cat, without a car, where her only phone is a landline.

Lucia Lemieux, MFA, is a retired English and creative writing teacher from Newbury Park High School where she advised the award-winning *Bold in Italics* literary magazine. She received the Nancy Bailey Human Rights Award from the California Teachers Association and the WHO Award from the Channel Island Service Center for her union advocacy. Recent poems have been featured in the *Midsummer Night's Dream Anthology* (Southern Arizona Press), *Herbs & Spices* (Highland Park Poetry Press), and *UPenn* (2024). She is a member of the Society of Children's Book Writers and Illustrators and the South Coast Writers Project.

Mari L'Esperance's collection of poems *The Darkened Temple* (University of Nebraska Press) was awarded a Prairie Schooner Book Prize in Poetry. An earlier collection, *Begin Here*, was awarded a Sarasota Poetry Theatre Press Chapbook Prize. With Tomás Q. Morín, she co-edited *Coming Close: Forty Essays on Philip Levine* (Prairie Lights Books / University of Iowa Press). Mari's poems are forthcoming in *Ploughshares* and the anthology *Twenty Years of PoemoftheWeek. com,* edited by Andrew McFayden-Ketchum.

Lori Levy's poems have appeared in *Rattle, Nimrod International Journal, Poet Lore, Paterson Literary Review*, and numerous other online and print literary journals in the U.S, the U.K, and Israel. Two of her chapbooks were published in 2023: *What Do You Mean When You Say Green? and Other Poems of Color* (Kelsay Books), and *Feet in L.A., But My Womb Lives in Jerusalem, My Breath in Vermont* (Ben Yehuda Press). Levy lives in Los Angeles with her husband, near her children and grandchildren.

Karen K. Lewis lives in rural Mendocino County. She's a longtime creative writing workshop leader with California Poets in the Schools and in other community settings. Her prose and poetry are included in anthologies and journals such as *Hip Mama, Literary Mama, Minerva Rising, Iron Horse,* and magazines for youth. Her most recent book is *Peace Maps* (Finishing Line Press).

Shirley Geok-lin Lim is winner of the Commonwealth Poetry Prize for *Crossing the Peninsula,* two American Book Awards, the Multiethnic Literatures of the United States (MELUS), and Feminist Press Lifetime Achievement Award. She has published in *Hudson Review, Feminist Studies, Virginia Quarterly Review, Jeal: Journal of Ethnic American Literature,* and others. Her memoir is *Among the White Moon Faces.* She has 12 poetry collections, most recently *In Praise of Limes* and *Dawns Tomorrow,* as well as three novels and three story collections.

Andrea Lingenfelter is a poet, award-winning Chinese-English literary translator, and fourth generation Californian. She has taught Chinese literature at UC Davis and a survey of contemporary literature and film of the Asia Pacific at the University of SF. Her poetry has appeared in *Plume* and *Asian CHA.* Her translations of poetry by Zhai Yongming (*The Changing Room,* Zephyr Press) and Wang Yin (*A Summer Day in The Company of Ghosts,* New York Review Books) won Northern California Book Awards.

Perie Longo, Santa Barbara Poet Laureate (2007-09), has published four books of poetry: *Milking the Earth, the Privacy of Wind, With Nothing Behind but Sky: a journey through grief,* and most recently, *Baggage Claim,* as well as poems in numerous poetry journals and anthologies. A Poet in the Schools for 25 years, she leads poetry workshops for the Santa Barbara Writers Conference as well as privately. Poetry Chair of the Nuclear Age Peace Foundation, she is also a psychotherapist who facilitates poetry writing for healing workshops at Santa Barbara Hospice.

Lisa Loop (MFA UCR/PD) is a poet, novelist, and essayist with a background in film. Her work appears in *NBC.com/THINK, The Coachella Review, Kelp Journal, Ballast Journal,* and other places. She lives in Los Angeles with her husband and their Aussie Shephard mix. One day she hopes to rent a house in the Baltic Archipelago and spend all summer writing, hunting for mushrooms, and floating.

Suzanne Lummis' fourth full-length collection, *Crime Wave,* is forthcoming from Giant Claw. She hosts a YouTube series exploring film noir and noir-themed poems, *They Write by Night,* which is produced by poetry.la, and also appears on YouTube. She is the editor of the Pacific Coast Poetry Series, an imprint of Beyond Baroque Books, and the editor of the national anthology, *Poetry Goes to the Movies.* She was a 2018/19 COLA (City of Los Angeles) Fellow in Poetry.

Glenna Luschei is a poet, publisher, editor, and philanthropist. She has been named a "Literary Treasure" by the Ventura County Poetry Project. Luschei is the author of multiple collections, most recently *Victory Garden* in 2023. Her imprint, Solo Press, has published books and journals for over fifty years.

Alison Luterman has published four previous collections of poetry, including *The Largest Possible Life, See How We Almost Fly, Desire Zoo*, and *In the Time of Great Fires*. In addition to poetry, she writes personal essays, plays, and song lyrics.

Ronna Magy is a Los Angeles-based poet. Her writing appears in *Rise Up Review, Writers Resist, The Los Angeles Press, The Cost of Our Baggage, Persimmon Tree, Sinister Wisdom,* and *Wild Crone Wisdom*. An alumna of the Napa Valley Writer's Conference, she was recently honored by West Hollywood as a civil rights hero. Ronna curates readings of seasoned queer women poets. She's a retired English as a Second Language instructor, textbook author, and staff development specialist.

devorah major is California born and raised, the granddaughter of immigrants, documented and undocumented. She was San Francisco's third Poet Laureate. A baker of pies and lover of jazz, she has seven books of poetry, two novels, *An Open Weave* and *Brown Glass Windows*, as well as poems, essays and short stories published in anthologies and periodicals. Her eighth book of poetry, *word time,* will be released by City Lights Press.

Eileen Malone is widely published. In addition to her many awards and citations, she founded and directed the Soul-Making Literary Competition. After 30 years of service, she has retired and is spending her days tending to her own craft in the coastal San Francisco Bay Area.

Ruthie Marlenée is a native Californian with Mexican roots. She earned a Writers' Certificate in Fiction from UCLA and is the author of *Isabela's Island, Curse of the Ninth*, and *Agave Blues,* which received an Honorable Mention from the International Latino Book Awards. Her writing has been nominated twice for the Pushcart Prize. She is a member of Macondo Writers Workshop, Inlandia Institute, Palm Springs Writers Guild, and is a WriteGirl Mentor. Her poetry and short stories can be found in various publications.

Seretta Martin is a Phillip Levine, Washington Prize, and *Atlantic Review* prize finalist. Her work has a appeared here and abroad in journals including *Patterson Review, Gyroscope, Poetry International, Web del Sol,* and others. She teaches at Oasis Learning Center and San Diego Writer's Ink and holds an MFA from SDSU. Her newest book is *Holographic Reality: Poems of an Eclectic Life* (Blue Vortex Publishers). She is Managing Editor of the *San Diego Poetry Annual.*

Lake McClenney is a clinical psychologist and psychotherapist whose poetry has appeared in SDPA. She has worked in a walnut factory and as a community activist, and has taught statistical analysis to unwilling psychology graduate students. As a second-generation Californian, the natural environment has been a lifelong source of solace, and now, of loss.

Kathleen McClung's books include *Questions of Buoyancy, A Juror Must Fold in on Herself* (winner of the Rattle Chapbook Prize), *The Typists Play Monopoly, Temporary Kin*, and *Almost the Rowboat.* Her poems appear widely in journals and anthologies. Winner of the Morton Marr, Maria W. Faust, and Rita Dove national poetry prizes, she was a 2024 finalist for San Francisco poet laureate. From 2021-23 she served as guest editor of *The MacGuffin.* She teaches at Skyline College, Osher Lifelong Learning Institute, and privately.

Mary Ann McFadden's first book, *Eye of the Blackbird*, won the Four Way Books Intro Prize in Poetry. *Devil, Dear,* McFadden's second book, was published in by Alice James Books. McFadden is a graduate of Occidental College and New York University. Her poetry has been published in local and national magazines and has been anthologized in collections by Scribner and Ballantine Books. She was awarded a MacDowell Fellowship. McFadden taught English and Poetry at Brooklyn College, City University of New York, and has recently been selected as Poet Laureate of Ventura County.

Anita McLaughlin works at Blanchard Community Library in Santa Paula, where she facilitates an open mic on the second Saturday of the month. She lives in Santa Paula on the edge of the Santa Clara River within the shadow of South Mountain. She often writes about wildlife in Heritage Valley. Her poems have been published in journals such as *SALT, SMC Emeritus Chronicles, Askew,* and *Canyon Chronicle*, and included in *Nuance: The VCWC Anthology* and *Out of the Ground, Poems Inspired by Santa Barbara Botanic Garden.*

Nancy L. Meyer is an intrepid cyclist, community activist, and educator from San Francisco. She's had two nominations each for Pushcart and Best of the Net. Her new poetry book is *The Stoop and The Steeple.* She's appeared in nine anthologies and many journals including *Anti-Heroin Chic, The Colorado Review, The Laurel Review*, and *Tupelo Quarterly*. She's the recipient of a Hedgebrook Residency.

Robin Michel was born in Utah and moved to Northern California at the age of seventeen. Her poetry and prose have appeared in many print and online journals. She is the author of the award-winning chapbook *Things Will Be Better in Bountiful* (Comstock Review) and one full-length collection, *Beneath a Strawberry Night Sky* (Raven & Wren Press). She lives in San Francisco.

Amy Michelson's work has appeared in *Talking River, Griffin, Sanskrit, Midwest Quarterly,* and many other journals and anthologies. A licensed Spiritual Practitioner, she lives in the mountains of Santa Barbara, California, with her husband. Amy leads monthly Sacred Sunday writing groups in Santa Barbara's Botanic Garden—think Forest Bathing with a pen!

Kathee Miller, a professor of depth psychology, has been writing as long as she can remember, from her origins in New York to California, bringing an embodied connection to memory and place. She is a passionate photographer and lives with her artist husband of 50 years in the Santa Barbara foothills near their son. Her poems appear in journals and books such as *While You Wait: Santa Barbara County Poets, Rare Feathers: Poetry on Birds and Art,* and *The Pepper Lane Review Vol. II: Poetry, Memoir, & Essay.*

Susan Miller has always loved playing with words. She has a created storybooks for her four amazing grandchildren with titles like *Hairy Larry, Adventures of Amatista in the Amazon* and *Pata the Penguin.* Susan is a retired speech therapist who lives with her husband in the hills of Los Angeles. She enjoys sharing her backyard with owls, coyotes, deer, hawks and bobcats and 18 different fruit trees.

Elaine Mintzer has published most recently in *Anacapa Review* and *Shiela-Na-Gig.* Her work has been featured on Moontide Press poet-of-the-month page, *Cultural Weekly, MacQueen's Quinterly, Beloit Poetry Review,* and elsewhere. Mintzer's first collection was *Natural Selections* (Bombshelter Press).

Penelope Moffet is the author of *Cauldron of Hisses* (Arroyo Seco Press), *It Isn't That They Mean to Kill You* (Arroyo Seco Press) and *Keeping Still* (Dorland Mountain Arts). Her poems have been published in *Afield, Eclectica, One by Jacar Press,* and other literary journals. A Pushcart Prize nominee, she lives in Southern California. A new collection will be published by Sheila-Na-Gig Editions in 2026.

Leslie Monsour is the author of *The Alarming Beauty of the Sky,* several chapbooks, *The Colosseum Critical Introduction to Rhina P. Espaillat,* and the forthcoming Kelsay Books collection, *Before the Forest Burns.* The recipient of five Pushcart Prize nominations and an NEA Fellowship, Monsour lives in Los Angeles, California, where she currently serves as Poet Laureate of Laurel Canyon.

Ruth Gunn Mota moved to Palo Alto California at age six and lived there until she attended Oberlin College. After college she joined the Peace Corps and moved to Brazil where she lived for a decade. She worked as an international health trainer before settling in the Santa Cruz Mountains where she now focuses on writing poetry and facilitating poetry groups in her community. Over 50 of her poems have been published in online and print journals.

Sharanya Naik is a high school teacher in San Francisco and a facilitator of Holotropic Breathwork. She has been writing and writing and writing for a long time, as well as singing, dancing, taking care of her daughter's cat, swimming, and generally trying to relax into a life with fewer high stakes.

Robbi Nester, a retired college educator, is the author of five books of poetry, including a forthcoming ekphrastic collection to be published by Shanti Arts. She curates and hosts two monthly Zoom poetry series: Verse-Virtual Monthly Poetry Reading and Words With You.

Gail Newman is a child of Polish Holocaust survivors, born in a Displaced Persons' Camp in Lansberg, Germany, before her family immigrated to Los Angeles. Her poems have appeared in *Prairie Schooner* and *The Atlanta Review* and in anthologies including *Ghosts of the Holocaust*, and *America, We Call Your Name*. Her poetry book is *One World* (Moon Tide Press). Her latest, *Blood Memory*, was chosen by Marge Piercy for the Marsh Hawk Press Poetry Prize, won the Northern California Authors and Publishers Gold Award for Poetry, and a Best Book Award. Gail lives in San Francisco and Sebastopol.

Kathy O'Fallon has been a Californian for over 50 years. She found poetry on the West Coast, all its beauty and heartache. Published in journals such as *Rattle, Gyroscope Review, Salt Marsh Press, LaDirge*, and others. She has been a finalist for three full-length manuscript awards and has had three chapbooks published. Grandmother of five girls, she is a psychologist in Carlsbad.

Jennifer O'Neill Pickering once danced with Allen Ginsburg. Her prose and poetry are published in print, audio, and nationwide. Her latest poetry book is *Fruit Box Castles: Poems from a Peach Rancher's Daughter* (Finishing Line Press*)*. She's a Pushcart Prize nominee and a finalist in the New Women's Voices Chapbook Competition. She received an Honorable Mention for the Craft First Chapters contest for her novel *Summer of the River Bottom Dragon*. Recent publications include prose in *Persimmon Tree*, and poetry in *California Quarterly, Moonstone Press*, and *Tule Review*. She lives in Sacramento with her musician husband and their daughter.

Dion O'Reilly is the author of *Sadness of the Apex Predator*, finalist for the Steel Toe Book Prize and the Ex Ophidia Prize; *Ghost Dogs*, winner of the Pinnacle Book Achievement Award, The Independent Press Award for Poetry; and *Limerence*, finalist for the John Pierce Chapbook Competition. Her work appears in *The Sun, Rattle, Cincinnati Review, The Slowdown*, and *Alaska Quarterly*. She facilitates workshops, hosts a podcast at The Hive Poetry Collective, and reads for *Catamaran Literary Quarterly*.

Enid Osborn has lived in Santa Barbara for 44 years and served as Poet Laureate from 2017-2019. Her book *When the Big Wind Comes* takes place in Southeast New Mexico, where her family raised quarter horses. Current projects include two books near completion, *Little Wakes* and *Pedregosa Street*. Her poems appear mainly in West Coast and Southwest journals and anthologies. She co-edited the anthology, *A Bird Black as the Sun / California Poets on Crows & Ravens*. In addition to poetry, she writes songs, stories and reviews. She is a visual artist and longtime advocate for preservation of bees.

Dairine Pearson grew up in Ireland and emigrated to California over 30 years ago. She graduated from UCSB and CSU Long Beach and is a Licensed Clinical Social Worker. Since 2010, she has been a full-time grief counselor for VNA Health, a home health and hospice care provider in Santa Barbara County. She enjoys writing, running, crafts and hiking our amazing coastline and mountains.

Christine Penko is the author of *Thunderbirds*, a memoir in poetry. Her most recent work can be found in *Prairie Schooner, Solo Voyage, SALT*, and the *International Poetry Anthology for Ukraine: And Blue Will Rise Over Yellow*. Christine also reviews poetry and, for 20 years, taught poetry in Santa Barbara's elementary schools with the statewide non-profit, California Poets in the Schools. Christine's interests include world affairs, her husband of 43 years, and learning to navigate the unexpectedly challenging terrain of life with adult children.

Ronna Perrin is 82 years old. She became hooked when writing her sixth-grade graduation play and she's been writing ever since. She uses prose poetry to dissect and better understand her experiences.

Penny Perry is a seven-time Pushcart Prize nominee. Her books are *Santa Monica Disposal and Salvage, The Woman With Newspaper Shoes,* and a novel, *Selling Pencils, and Charlie,* a San Diego Book Awards finalist. She was prose editor at *Knot Literary Magazine* for 10 years. One of the first female screenwriting fellows at the American Film Institute, a screenplay she wrote there became a film on PBS. Her work has appeared in many publications including *Lilith, Poetry International, San Diego Poetry Annual*, and *Paterson Literary Review*.

Lois Phillips, Ph.D., is a retired university administrator and organizational development consultant to colleges and universities. She has been a conference speaker, author, and executive coach. She has written opinion essays about gender and rhetoric and women advancing into leadership and political roles. She has taught communication workshops for years and now, as a "student," enjoys regular workshops with poet Perie Longo. She has two middle-aged "children" living in the Bay Area and is married to a Santa Barbara architect. Phillips has received several awards as an advocate for working women.

Evelyn Jean Pine is a poet, playwright, performer, and PlayGround June Ann Baker Prize winner. Her play *Freeloader in the House of Love* won the "Most Compelling Story" prize at Boulder Fringe. *The Invisible Project*, co-written with Katja Rivera, launched the Latinx Mafia's staged reading series. Her short opera, *nada*, written with Norwegian composer, Tze Yeung Ho, premiered at Strange Trace Opera's Stencils Festival. Her comedy, *7 Secrets of Teaching Online*, developed during a 2020 PlayGround Residency, was the hit of Theatre 33's 2022 New Works Festival.

Kathy Pon earned a doctorate in education, but in retirement turned to her life-long passion for writing poetry. Her husband is a third-generation farmer, and they live in an almond orchard. As a native Californian she is constantly inspired by the state's natural landscape. Her poems have been/will be featured in *Eunoia Review, Penumbra, Passengers Journal, Canary, RockPaperPoem*, and others.

Connie Post served as Poet Laureate of Livermore. Her work has appeared in *Calyx, Cutthroat, River Styx, Slipstream, Spoon River Poetry Review*, and elsewhere. Her awards include the Crab Creek Poetry Prize, Liakoura Award and the Caesura Poetry Award. Her second full length book, *Prime Meridian* (Glass Lyre Press), was a finalist for the Best Book Awards. Her most recent books are *Between Twilight* (New York Quarterly Books) and *Broken Metronome* (Glass Lyre Press), which won the American Fiction Award for poetry chapbook.

Sharon Pretti lives in San Francisco. Her work has appeared in numerous journals including *Calyx, The MacGuffin, Spillway, The Bellevue Literary Review*, and *Canary*. She has received multiple Pushcart Prize nominations and was selected for the Best New Poets 2024 anthology. She is an award-winning haiku poet and frequent contributor to haiku journals including *Modern Haiku* and *Frogpond*. Sharon is a retired medical social worker and taught poetry workshops in a nursing home and at assisted living facilities in the San Francisco Bay Area.

Anita S. Pulier's chapbooks *Perfect Diet, The Lovely Mundane* and *Sounds of Morning*, and her books, *The Butcher's Diamond* and *Toast* are from Finishing Line Press. Kelsay Books published her book *Paradise Reexamined* and her latest book, *Leaving Brooklyn*. Anita's poems have appeared in many journals and her work is included in several print anthologies. Anita has been a featured poet on *The Writer's Almanac* and *Cultural Daily*.

Peg Quinn's poetry and non-fiction have been published in numerous journals and anthologies and four times nominated for the Pushcart Prize. Her debut poetry collection, *Mother Lode*, was published by Gunpowder Press.

Kathryn Ridall's work has appeared in dozens of journals and anthologies. She has published three chapbooks, two poetry anthologies, and an award-winning book on dreaming. Her full-length collection, *The Living Waters Between Us*, is forthcoming from Kelsay Books. She lives in Ventura where she works as a psychotherapist.

Lisa Rosenberg is the author of *A Different Physics* (Red Mountain Press), winner of the American Legacy Book Award for Poetry. A former space program engineer trained as a physicist, her work has been recognized by a Djerassi Leonardo Residency, Wallace Stegner Fellowship, and MOSAIC America Fellowship. She served as Poet Laureate of San Mateo County and is a frequent speaker on the confluence of arts and sciences. Her poems and multidisciplinary essays appear in venues such as *The Threepenny Review, Plume, Poetry, SWWIM*, and the collection *California Fire & Water: A Climate Crisis Anthology*.

Mary Kay Rummel is enjoying reading from her tenth poetry book, a collection of new and selected poems, *Little River of Amazements* (Blue Light Press). Previous books have won awards from New Rivers Press, Bright Hill Press, and Blue Light Press. She is professor emerita from the University of Minnesota and taught at California State University, Channel Islands. She divides her time between St. Paul, Minnesota, and Ventura, and she was Poet Laureate of Ventura County.

Beth Ruscio is the author of *Speaking Parts* (2020), winner of The Brick Road Poetry Prize. Also an award-winning actor on stages & screens, she comes from a California family of artists, actors, teachers & writers. Her poems & essays are included in *Outlaw Theatre* (Padua Playwrights Press), *Poetry Goes To The Movies* (Beyond Baroque), *Dark Ink: Poetry Inspired By Horror* (Mood Tide Press).

Sue Sesnon Salt is a fourth-generation Californian. She is now retired and has the time to pursue her writing. Her short essay "Calling my Muse" was recently published on the *Brevity Blog*. Her essay "On Not Belonging" is forthcoming in *Persimmon Tree*.

Renée M. Schell's debut collection is *Overtones* (Tourane Poetry Press). Her poetry appears in *New Verse News, Catamaran Literary Reader, Literary Mama, Naugatuck River Review*, and many other journals. She was lead editor for the anthology *(AFTER)life: Poems and Stories of the Dead*. She holds a Ph.D. in German Studies and taught for seven years at a Title I elementary school in San José. Her work has been nominated for Best of the Net.

Linda Scheller is a retired educator and the author of two books of poetry, *Fierce Light* (FutureCycle Press) and *Wind & Children* (Main Street Rag). She serves as vice president of Modesto-Stanislaus Poetry Center and programs for KCBP Community Radio.

Carla Schick is a queer, nonbinary social justice activist. Their writings are inspired by the complexities of jazz to get at emotions in the intersections of political and personal events. Their writings can be found in *Sinister Wisdom, Fourteen*

Hills, Black Fox Literary Magazine, Qu, and anthologized in *Colossus: Body.* They are a 2023 recipient of a SF Foundation/Nomadic Press Literary Award. They are forever grateful to the professors at Berkeley City College with whom they studied, earning a Certificate in Poetry.

Claire Scott is an award-winning poet who has received multiple Pushcart Prize nominations. Her work has appeared in the *Atlanta Review, Bellevue Literary Review, New Ohio Review* and *Healing Muse,* among other journals. Scott is the author of *Waiting to be Called* and *Until I Couldn't.* She is the co-author of *Unfolding in Light: A Sisters' Journey in Photography and Poetry.*

Anna Scotti's first collection, *Bewildered by All This Broken Sky,* was awarded the inaugural Lightscatter Prize and was a finalist for several other awards including the Housatonic Book Award, the CPR Editor's Prize, and the Anthony Hecht Poetry Prize. Her poetry can be found in a variety of literary journals, including *The New Yorker, Nimrod,* and *Chautauqua.* Scotti is also a noted mystery writer and an award-winning young adult author. She teaches poetry, fiction, and creative nonfiction at writers.com.

Linda Serrato is a native Californian and a retired dual immersion teacher. She has been writing poetry close to 40 years. She is inspired by nature, her family and the talented scribes of her writing groups. Her work has been published in *Watershed Literary Review, Sacred Stone, Sacred Wate*r and *Sisters Singing: Blessings, Prayers, Art, Songs, Poetry and Sacred Stories by Women.*

Joanne Sharp is a native Southern Californian who has spent her life near the coast. She has a BA in Art and Design from UCLA. Her career in graphic design, visual and textile arts has been balanced with interests in music and literature. For the last decade, poetry has been her main creative focus. Publications include the *San Diego Poetry Annual, Escondido Arts Partners Summation,* and *California Quarterly,* among others.

Mara Teitel Sheade's poems have appeared in *Pandemic Puzzle Poems, The Paterson Literary Review, Voices of the Grieving Heart* and elsewhere. She has taught poetry and creative writing in a variety of community settings, including schools, libraries, and Senior Centers, and lives in the San Francisco Bay Area.

Joan Jobe Smith is the founding editor of *PEARL* literary journal (1974-2017) and *Bukowski Review* (2001-2006). A graduate of UC Irvine with an MFA in Fiction, she has been published internationally in more than 1000 journals, anthologies, newspapers, and magazines. Her most recent publications include *Made in the Shade* (UK's Tangerine Press), *Moonglow a Go-Go* (NYQ), *Tales of An Ancient Go-Go Girl, a Memoir* (MarJo Books) and *Charles Bukowski: Epic Glottis: His Art & His Women (& me)* (Silver Birch Press).

Dale Griffiths Stamos is an award-winning screenwriter, director, and producer. Her poetry has been published in such journals as *Calyx, Rattle*, and *ONTHEBUS*. She has written and produced or co-produced six short films—three of which she directed—which have been official selections at over 70 film festivals, including Palms Springs Shortfest, LA Shorts International and Dances with Films. She is currently in post-production with her first feature film, *Imbalance*, which she wrote, directed and produced. It stars Emmy-nominated actress Sharon Lawrence and star of "The Good Doctor," Nicholas Gonzalez.

Jan Steckel's debut fiction collection is *Ghosts and Oceans* (Zeitgeist Press). Her poetry book *The Horizontal Poet* (Zeitgeist Press) won a Lambda Literary Award. Her poetry book *Like Flesh Covers Bone* (Zeitgeist Press) won two Rainbow Awards. Her fiction chapbook *Mixing Tracks* (Gertrude Press) and poetry chapbook *The Underwater Hospital* (Zeitgeist Press) also won awards. Her creative prose and poetry have appeared in *Scholastic Magazine, Yale Medicine, Bellevue Literary Review, Canary,* and elsewhere. She lives in Oakland.

Jeanine Stevens' latest books are *Left Handed Hummingbird* (Clare Songbirds Publishing) and a chapbook, *Tea in the Nun's Library* (Eyewear Publishing, UK). She won the MacGuffin Poet Hunt, the Ekphrasis Prize, and the William Stafford Award. *Gertrude Sitting: Portraits of Women* won the Heartland Review Chapbook Contest. Her publications include *Evansville Review, North Dakota Review, Chiron Review, Clackamas Literary Review,* and others. Professor Emerita at American River College, she studied poetry at UC Davis, received her M.A. at CSU Sacramento and has a doctorate in Education. Raised in Indiana, she lives with her husband Greg Chalpin in Northern California.

Patti Sullivan's poetry books are *At The Booth Memorial Home for Unwed Mothers* 1966, *Not Fade Away,* and *For The Day*. Individual poems appear in *Spillway, Chiron Review, Solo, Raising Lilly Ledbetter, Askew* and other journals and anthologies. Her artwork appears in numerous books and journals. She is a native Californian, self-taught artist and poet living on the Central Coast.

Stephanie Taylor was born in Chico. She's a visual storyteller and environmental writer merging four decades of large-scale mural and sculpture installations with environmentally focused essays, art, and photography. Her series "California Sketches" for the *Sacramento Bee* blended art and non-fiction. She has co-authored three books: *Water: More or Less, A Graphic Interpretation of Frankenstein,* and *Simple Objects*. She's the mother of three, grandmother of eight, and happy ex-wife.

Nancy Weaver Teichert was a national award-winning investigative journalist for 30 years. Her reporting on inadequate public schools garnered the Pulitzer

Prize for Public Service for the Jackson, MS, *Clarion-Ledger*. At the *Denver Post* and *Sacramento Bee*, she exposed public corruption, racism, poverty, elder abuse, and the deaths of children under county care. An active community volunteer in Sacramento, she now writes historical and creative nonfiction and attends every summer workshop.

Lynne Thompson served as Los Angeles' 4th Poet Laureate and received a Poet Laureate Fellowship from the Academy of American Poets. She is the author of four collections of poetry, most recently *Blue on a Blue Palette* (BOA Editions). Thompson is the recipient of multiple awards, including the George Drury Smith Award for Outstanding Achievement in Poetry. Thompson's recent work can be found or is forthcoming in the literary journals *Best American Poetry 2020, Kenyon Review, Georgia Review, Copper Nickel*, and *Gulf Coast*.

Carine Topal, born and raised in NYC, holds an MA from New York University. She has been awarded residencies in the U.S. and Russia, is the recipient of poetry awards including the Robert G. Cohn Prose Poetry Award and the Briar Cliff Poetry Award, Red Wheelbarrow Poetry Prize, and others. Her chapbook, *Tattooed,* won the Palettes and Quills Poetry Chapbook Contest. Topal's 5th collection, *In Order of Disappearance*, is part of Beyond Baroque's Pacific Coast Poetry Series. Topal's newest book is *Dear Blood* (Ben Yehuda Press). She lives in Southern California with her husband and leads poetry and memoir workshops.

Terra Trevor is the author of *We Who Walk the Seven Ways: A Memoir* (University of Nebraska Press). She lives in Santa Cruz, California.

Alison Turner is the author of *The Second Split Between* (selected by Dorianne Laux for the Catamaran Poetry Prize for West Coast Poets) and the chapbook, *What To Do In An Emergency*. Her poems have appeared in various literary journals and anthologies, including, *The American Journal of Poetry, Hudson Review, Mid-American Review, Nimrod, Catamaran Literary Reader,* and *California Fire & Water, A Climate Crisis Anthology*, Molly Fisk ed. (Story Street Press). She lives in Los Angeles under the Hollywood sign.

Georgette Unis is the author of two books—*Watercolors in the Desk Drawer* and *Tremors*—both published by Finishing Line Press. Several literary journals also published her poems. A painter as well as a poet, she resides in the Sierra foothills of northern California.

Patrice Vecchione is the author of three books of nonfiction, most recently, *My Shouting, Shattered, Whispering Voice: A Guide to Writing Poetry & Speaking Your Truth*.She has two collections of poems and is the editor of many anthologies, inclucing *Ink Knows No Borders: Poems of the Immigrant and Refugee Experience*. She leads writing workshops along the Central Coast and elsewhere.

Erie Vitiello, a transplant from the Deep South, has lived in Davis for 34 years. She holds a B.A. in Art History from Swarthmore College, an M.S. in Dance Therapy from Hahnemann University, and an M.A. in Creative Writing from UC Davis. Her story "Chasing the Rain" appeared in *THEMA* and her novel, *Letters South*, was a finalist for the Heekin Foundation's James Fellowship for the Novel in Progress. Currently retired, she has been a psychiatric dance therapist, a university writing instructor, and a nonprofit arts administrator.

Charlotte Ward, co-authored *The Home Birth Book* (Doubleday); *Simply Live It Up: Brief Solutions* (Purposeful Press); and a series on gemology (Gem Book Publishers). She is editor of numerous books. Ward and her son are collaborating on a poetry/photographic art book, *Atmosphere: Infinite Malibu*. With a BA in English (University of Florida) and an MLS with Distinction (Georgetown University), she is credentialed in Myers-Briggs Type Indicator, Neuro-Linguistic Programing, and Photo Reading. A member of Malibu Woman's Club, Ward also hosts a weekly women's writing group and the open Malibu-Ventura Vital Poetry.

Wendy Watson was born in Pasadena. Her family moved to Balboa Island when she was three years old. The family camped on the beaches and in forests up and down the coast and in Yosemite, Death Valley, and Baja California. They moved to northern California when she was fifteen. She graduated from UC Berkeley in 1970 and returned to school in the 1980s to earn a Masters degree in counseling. She retired from private practice in Davis. Her most recent adventure was to walk the Camino Frances in Spain.

Florence Weinberger is the author of six published collections of poetry. The most recent, *These Days of Simple Mooring*, won the Blue Light Book Award. Five times nominated for a Pushcart Prize, and Best of the Net, her poetry has appeared in *The Comstock Review, Nimrod, Poetry East, Rattle, The Los Angeles Review*, and other journals. Poems have also been published in anthologies, including, *The New Los Angeles Poets, So Luminous the Wildflowers*, and *The Widows' Handbook*.

Hilda Weiss lives in California where she was born in 1948. Her poetry has been published in journals such as *Rattle, Cultural Daily, Poet Lore*, and *Spillway*, as well as in anthologies such as *Wide Awake: Poets of Los Angeles* and *Coiled Serpent*. Her chapbook is *Optimism About Trees*. Her full-length manuscript, *Seemingly Normal*, was a finalist in the National Federation of State Poetry Societies competition. She is the co-founder and curator for www.Poetry.LA, a website that features videos of poets and poetry venues in Southern California.

Carol Ann Wilburn started writing poetry at a young age, a practice she has continued throughout her life. Her poems were published in *While You Wait: A Collection of Santa Barbara Poets* (Gunpowder Press), *Live Encounters Poetry*

& Writing, in the *Bryant Literary Review*, and in *Our California*, a joint project of California Poet Laureate Lee Herrick and the California Arts Council. Additionally, her poem, "My Piano Man", was the winner of the Carol DeCanio Abeles Emerging Poets Prize.

Kimberly Wiley, MD, is a San Franciscan native and graduate of the University of San Francisco and UC San Diego School of Medicine. Retired in 2022, she practiced family medicine for 29 years, the last 22 at Kaiser Permanente. She lives in Sacramento and pens flash fiction and poetry. Her publications include the poem "Water, Water Everywhere…" in the virtual *North Bay Poetics Anthology*, a short story in the mystery collection *Obsidian Tales* (edited by Boranda Diaz), and two flash fiction stories in the *San Joaquin Valley Writers* inaugural anthology.

Sharon M. Williams is an author, poet, and teacher in the greater Los Angeles area. She is the author of two poetry collections and is currently working on a nonfiction book. Sharon also facilitates a women's writing group, which she loves, and she strives to inspire and support writers of all genres.

Maw Shein Win's second poetry collection is *Percussing the Thinking Jar* (Omnidawn). Her first collection, *Storage Unit for the Spirit House* (Omnidawn), was nominated for the Northern California Book Award in Poetry, longlisted for the PEN America Open Book Award, and shortlisted for the Golden Poppy Award for Poetry. Her work has been published in *The American Poetry Review, The Margins, The Bangalore Review*, and other journals. She is the inaugural poet laureate of El Cerrito, CA. She teaches poetry in the MFA Program at USF and is a member of The Writers Grotto.

Terry Wolverton is author of 12 books of poetry, fiction and creative nonfiction, including *Embers*, a novel in poems; *Insurgent Muse: art and life at the Woman's Building,* a memoir; and her most recent novel, *Season of Eclipse*. She has also edited 16 literary compilations. She is the founder of Writers At Work, a creative writing studio in Los Angeles, and Affiliate Faculty in the MFA Writing Program at Antioch University Los Angeles.

Susan Woolridge's book *poemcrazy: freeing your life with words* (Crown/Random) is now past its 30th printing. *Poets and Writers* has sponsored Susan's workshops in over 80 rural libraries in California. Susan has a chapbook of poems, *Bathing with Ants*, and a book about creative process, *Foolsgold: Making Something from Nothing*. Susan is now writing about land and language from a vintage trailer named the Bolt on a burned down ranch.

Gail Wronsky is the author of eight books of poetry, three coauthored collections of experimental poetry, and two books of translations of the poetry of Argentinean poet Alicia Partnoy. Her newest book is a chapbook of poems called

Some Disenfranchised Evening, winner of the Swan Scythe Chapbook Prize. Other books include *The Stranger You Are*, with artwork by the renowned artist Gronk (Tía Chucha Press), *Dying for Beauty* (Copper Canyon) and *Under the Capsized Boat We Fly: New & Selected Poems* (White Pine Press). The recipient of an Artists Fellowship from the California Arts Council, Gail lives in Topanga.

Andrena Zawinski's poetry has received accolades for free verse, lyricism, form, nature, and social concern. She has published four full-length poetry collections along with some smaller editions, edited two anthologies, and authored a book of flash fictions. Her poetry has appeared widely in fine publications including *Aeolian Harp, Caesura, Gulf Coast, Rattle*, and others. Born and raised landlocked in Pittsburgh, Pennsylvania, she now makes her home at water's edge beneath a Pacific flyway on the city island of Alameda. Her most recent book of poetry is *Born Under the Influence.*

The following poems previously appeared in other publications:

"As Long as She Likes" by Ellen Bass first appeared in *The New Yorker* (April 11, 2022), Reprinted with permission of the poet.

"Living Kintsugi" by Kim Birdsong first appeared in the self-published *Rain to Root, poems of meeting grief and grace* (Nov 2024, Sage & Stone Press, Carmel, CA). Reprinted with permission of the poet.

"Pieces" by Sheryl J. Bize-Boutte appeared in *Traipsing In Poetry Prose and Vignette* (Fall 2024). Reprinted with permission of the poet.

"Farmer's Market in Antwerp" by Laure-Anne Bosselaar first appeared in *Vox Populi* (Fall 2024). Reprinted with permission of the poet.

"Does God Visit Santa Barbara?" by Valerie Anne Burns is excerpted from book and published in *Rituals*, 2023.

"The sound of stars crumbling without any malice/ In a corner of the universe..." by Elena Karina Byrne first appeared in *Anacapa Review*, Vol. 1, No. 9 (2023).

"The Wild Turkeys of Las Canoas" by Susan Chiavelli first appeared in *San Pedro River Review* (Vol. 10 No. 2, Fall 2018).

"Adam and Eve Near Retirement" by Susan Cohen first appeared in *A Different Wakeful Animal* (Red Dragonfly Press, 2016), winner of the 2015 David Martinson-Meadowhawk Prize. Reprinted with permission of the poet.

"Love Note" by Jean Colonomos includes an epigraph from *The Baseball 100*, by Joe Posnanski (Avid Reader Press, 2021).

"Slippery Slope" by Alexis Rhone Fancher was first published in *MacQueen's Quinterly* and was nominated for a Pushcart Prize in 2025. Reprinted with permission of the poet.

"Department of Complaint" by Laurel Feigenbaum appears in *The Daily Absurd*.

"California Dreaming" by Rebecca Foust was first published in the *Massachusetts Review*, Summer 2014, Vol 55:3 under the title "Dream of the Rood."

"The day my fallopian tubes asked me to play hopscotch" by Dianna Henning first appeared in *The Power of the Feminine* Vol.II, 2024. Reprinted with permission of the poet.

"What Eve Told the Snake" by Leslie Hodge first appeared in *Whale Road Review* (Spring 2024). Reprinted with permission of the poet.

"The Coming of...A Certain Age" by Elizabeth Iannaci appeared in *Interlitq* (California Poets: Part 6). Reprinted with permission of the poet.

"Rocketdyne, 1959" by Bonnie S. Kaplan was published in *The Northridge Review*. 2019.

"Fire Drill (Santa Rosa, California, 2017)" by Ellen Girardeau Kempler first appeared in *Tiny Seed Literary Journal* (December 2020) and is included in the chapbook,"Fire in My Head / Flame in My Heart: Poems for the Pyrocene" (Kelsay Books, 2025). Reprinted with permission of the poet.

"Are We Aging Out Of This Scene?" by Blair Kilpatrick first appeared in *Wild Greens Magazine* (Volume 5, Issue 4, February 2025.) Reprinted with the permission of the poet.

"Winter Wallop" by Veronica Kornberg was published in *Poet Lore, Vol. 119* (Summer/Fall 2024)

"1958 Fruit Cutting Shed" by Jennifer Lagier was published in *Boomer Girls* (University of Iowa Press, 1999).

"Joan of California" by Sheree La Puma was first published in *Juxtaprose Literary Magazine* (Volume 21, Fall 2019).

"The Way I See It" by Diane Lefer first appeared in *El Portal* (Spring 2015) and was included in *Waves: A confluence of women's voices* (AROHO, 2023).

"Taking Selfies with My Older Sister During Spring Thaw in Minnesota" by Perie Longo first appeared in *Passager* (Contest Issue #75, Spring 2023). Reprinted with permission of the poet.

"Listen Baby-Boomers" by Seretta Martin appears in *Holographic Reality: Poems of an Eclectic Life* (Blue Vortex Publishers, 2024).

"Knowledge and Praxis" by Kathleen McClung first appeared in *Marin Poetry Center Anthology 2024*. Reprinted with permission of the poet.

"Imagine" by Mary Ann McFadden was published in *Hanging Loose*, 115.

"All I Want, An Ecstatic Death" by Nancy L. Meyer appeared in *Caesura*, 2017.

"Forbidding Fruit" by Leslie Monsour first appeared in *The Rotary Dial* (December 2014). Reprinted with permission of the poet.

"Water Lessons" by Ruth Gunn Mota first appeared in *Nature of Our Times,* 2025. Reprinted with permission of the poet.

"California" by Robbi Nester was published at *MacQueen's Quinterly 17* (Jan. 2023).

"The Skater Lusts" by Evelyn Jean Pine first appeared in *No Crime in Rhymin'* on Medium (October 26, 2021). Reprinted with permission of the poet.

"Create a Revolution" by Diana Raab first published in *Verse-Virtual* (March 2025). Reprinted with permission of the poet.

"Citrus" by Lisa Rosenberg appeared in *SWWIM*, May 8, 2024.

"Highway 101" by Joanne Sharp is included in Lee Herrick's online anthology "Our California."

"Getting Drunk With My Third Mother-in-Law" by Joan Jobe Smith was published in *Best of California Women Poets, 1977*.

"An American Indian Elderhood in Calfornia" by Terra Trevor includes a portion of an essay adapted from *We Who Walk the Seven Ways: A Memoir by Terra Trevor*, by permission of the University of Nebraska Press. Copyright 2023 by the Board of Regents of the University of Nebraska.

"Catalog" by Maw Shein Win appears in *Percussing the Thinking Jar* (Omnidawn, 2024).

Diana Raab, MFA, Ph.D., is a poet, memoirist, workshop leader, and award-winning author of 14 books and the editor of three anthologies. Her work has been widely published and anthologized, and she's been nominated for the Pushcart Prize and The Best of the Net. She frequently speaks and writes on writing for healing and transformation. Her work has been published in *Rattle, Verse-Virtual, Vox Populi, New York Quarterly, SALT*, and others. Her latest book is *Hummingbird: Messages from My Ancestors* (2024). Raab writes for *Psychology Today, The Good Men Project, Sixty and Me, Medium*, and is a guest writer for many others.

Chryss Yost, Ph.D., is co-editor of Gunpowder Press and a Santa Barbara Poet Laureate. Her collection *Mouth & Fruit* was one of the books that launched Gunpowder Press. She is one of the editors of *California Poetry: From the Gold Rush to the Present*, published by Heyday Books. Her poems have been widely anthologized and published in journals including *Solo, SALT, Tule Review, Hudson Review*, among others. A SCAD heart attack survivor, she encourages everyone to be sure they recognize the signs of a heart attack.

Mary Heebner (cover artist) earned her BFA in Art and Literature from College of Creative Studies, and an MFA at UCSB. Heebner's recent collages transpose figures from antiquity in fresh and provocative ways. Simplemente Maria Press, founded by Heebner in 1995, will publish her new book, *Mythos Quartet,* in 2026. She and her husband, photographer Macduff Everton, live in Santa Barbara.

GUNPOWDER PRESS

SHORELINE VOICES SERIES
celebrating poetic voices in our community

Women in a Golden State:
California Poets at 60 and Beyond
Edited by Diana Raab & Chryss Yost

Out of the Ground:
Poems Inspired by Santa Barbara Botanic Garden
Edited by David Starkey & Chryss Yost

While You Wait:
A Collection by Santa Barbara County Poets
Edited by Laure-Anne Bosselaar

To Give Life a Shape:
Poems Inspired by the Santa Barbara Museum of Art
Edited by David Starkey & Chryss Yost

What Breathes Us:
Santa Barbara Poets Laureate, 2005-2015
Edited by David Starkey

Rare Feathers: Poems on Birds & Art
Edited by Nancy Gifford, Chryss Yost,
& George Yatchisin

Buzz: Poets Respond to SWARM
Edited by Nancy Gifford & Chryss Yost

GUNPOWDER PRESS

CALIFORNIA POETS SERIES

In Praise of Late Wonder, poems by Lee Herrick

Downtime, poems by Gary Soto

Speech Crush, poems by Sandra McPherson

Our Music, poems by Dennis Schmitz

Gatherer's Alphabet, poems by Susan Kelly-DeWitt

ALTA CALIFORNIA CHAPBOOKS

EMMA TRELLES, SERIES EDITOR

Alba and Other Songs, poems by Fred Arroyo

The First Amelia, poems by Amelia Rodriguez

On Display, poems by Gabriel Ibarra

Sor Juana, poems by Florencia Milito

Levitations, poems by Nicholas Reiner

Grief Logic, poems by Crystal AC Salas

COMPLETE CATALOG ONLINE AT GUNPOWDERPRESS.COM

www.ingramcontent.com/pod-product-compliance
Lightning Source LLC
Chambersburg PA
CBHW020233130626
46549CB00005B/1875